Island Tourism

Island Tourism

Harish Bhatt
B.S. Badan

CRESCENT
PUBLISHING CORPORATION

Island Tourism

First Published : 2006

ISBN 81-8342-008-7

Published by :

CRESCENT PUBLISHING CORPORATION
4831/24, Prahlad Street,
Ansari Road, Darya Ganj,
New Delhi - 110002
Ph. : 23272541, 23257835
Fax : 91- 011- 23257835
e-mail : campusbooks@hotmail.com

Typesetting by :

Arjun Computers
Delhi - 110051

Printed at :
Roshan Offset Printers
Delhi

Preface

Tourism is often identified as a promising growth sector in small island developing states. The most important tourism resources are the natural beauty of the island, their distinctive or exotic character, their recreation possibilities, and the cultural interest of the people. Tourism plays a dominant role in the economic well being of Small Island Tourism Economies (SITEs), and tourism earnings account for a significant proportion of the value added in their national product. The fundamental aim of tourism development in SITEs is to increase foreign exchange earnings to finance imports.

Though its enormous growth brings tremendous benefits in small islands, tourism also brings considerable threats to the environment in its broad sense, including the natural, social and built environment. Many deficits in the field of tourism such as the lack of standardization of definitions, market research and planning, adequate policies and legislation, information on tourism's possible implications and cooperation between key players have been aggravated by exponential and often uncontrolled growth. The continuing challenge for small islands is to establish the appropriate balance between tourism development and that of other sectors of the economy, given the limits of their carrying capacity and the fact that the tourism sector places demands on other sectors of the economy.

The present volume discusses the opportunities and challenges of tourism development in small islands. It will be a valuable reference tool for all concerned.

Harish Bhatt

B.S. Badan

Contents

1

Prospects of Island Tourism

The postwar history of small islands has been marked by two favorable development factors: the march of decolonization and the global spread of international tourism.

In the first case, since 1960 roughly 30 tropical/temperate islands across the five major oceanic basins have become politically independent. Other island territories have achieved significantly greater internal self-government and have used this new-found autonomy—the so called "resource of jurisdiction"—to create tax havens and diversify into other nontraditional activities like off-shore finance and ship registry.

In the second case, the remarkable transformation of tourism into the world's largest industry—accounting for roughly a tenth of global GDP, employment and capital formation—has coincided with the restructuring of small island economies away from traditional exports like sugar and copra toward mass tourism and related construction. The results have transformed insular landscapes across the Caribbean, Mediterranean and North Pacific and created the so-called "Pleasure Periphery" of North America, Europe and Japan respectively.

However, much of this growth has been overly rapid, unplanned and intrusive and has damaged insular ecosystems. In the Caribbean, tourism expansion has directly or indirectly caused deforestation and erosion of upland forests for condominium developments and road works, as well as beach loss, lagoon pollution and reef damage from sand mining, dredging and boat anchoring. Nearly 30 percent of the reefs are at high risk because of runoff and discharges of untreated municipal and hotel waste and pollution from pleasure yachts and cruise ships. Partly as a result, since 1985 fish catches are off nearly 50 percent in gross tonnage.

In the Mediterranean, large-scale coastal hotel/marina and infrastructure construction has filled in salt ponds, disfigured shorelines, and polluted nearshore waters with sewage. In highly developed islands like Balearics and Malta, tourism has been associated with the rapid decline of traditional pursuits and renewable resource uses, the rise of realty inflation, and paralyzing summer crowding and other sociocultural intrusions that threaten insular lifestyles and identity.

In developing Indian Ocean islands, the situation is similar. Tourism along with unplanned urbanization is associated with sand mining, mangrove destruction and coastal pollution. Mauritius and Seychelles are ranked second and third in the world in terms of endangered native plant species, and some beach-based resorts are under threat from sea level rise.

The Pacific, in transition from subsistence to a cash economy, is undergoing substantial threats from commercial agriculture and fishing, logging and coastal tourist development. In popular resort areas delicate mangroves have been harvested for construction material and reefs scarred by trampling and collecting by tourists. Development on Guam has been compared to suburban Los Angeles, and even the Galapagos has allegedly been overrun by excessive visitation. As a result of these forces of modernization, the region boasts the largest number of bird extinctions in the world, and seven times more endangered species than the Caribbean.

Since tourism's biocultural base is in decline across the island world, and because of the continued pressures from increased globalization expected for the future, researchers have called for greener, lower-density tourism styles and begun to explore the causes of this policy failure.

A variety of structural and institutional factors have been suggested: the disequilibrium between a large-scale consumption-based international tourist economy imposed upon a small island ecology; island policy makers' preoccupation with raising visitor numbers instead of net expenditure; tourism's asymmetrical dynamics whereby linear economic benefits are mismatched with non-linear socio-environmental costs; and the absence of a comprehensive measure of overall tourism impact, i.e. an early warning signal to broadly assess the approach of potentially dangerous socio-environmental thresholds.

Tourist Arrivals

Tourism plays a dominant role in the economic well being of Small Island Tourism Economies (SITEs), and tourism earnings account for a significant proportion of the value added in their national product. The fundamental aim of tourism development in SITEs is to increase foreign exchange earnings to finance imports. These SITEs have an overwhelming reliance on service industries, of which tourism accounts for the highest proportion in export earnings.

In economic planning, tourism has a predominant emphasis in SITEs where the climate is well suited for tourism development and the islands are strategically located. The square of the deviation from the mean of a GDP growth rate is known as the volatility of GDP growth. In SITEs, the volatility of GDP growth rate tends to be very high. Shareef calculated the real GDP growth rate and its volatility for 20 SITEs. Malta in the Mediterranean recorded the lowest mean volatility for the period 1980-2002, while St. Lucia in the Caribbean Sea recorded the highest mean volatility of 56.9 for the same period.

SITEs need a consistent inflow of foreign capital to smooth out consumption over the long run, while compensating for any adverse shocks to domestic production. A common feature of SITEs is that they depend heavily on foreign aid to finance development. Aid flows have dropped sharply during the last decade of the 20 th Century, due to the collapse of communism in Europe. Aid from donor countries has been diverted towards former Soviet allies. SITEs have experienced a dramatic decline in per capita aid of around US$145 in 1990 to less than US$ 100 per capita in 2000. They have very limited access to commercial borrowings because these are perceived to suffer from frequent natural disasters or for other reasons considered to be high risk.

Although SITEs have achieved high average per capita GDP relative to the larger developing countries, poverty continues to be an unabated challenge. Generally, with the increase in per capita GDP, there has been a decline in poverty. However, there are a number of small economies that have higher poverty rates than reflected in their per capita incomes, primarily because SITEs are island archipelagos. In such archipelagos, a large proportion of economic activity is confined to the capital, while the dispersed communities remain poor. Poverty prevalence becomes high with the uneven distribution of income. The high volatility of GDP, together with the population's inability to absorb negative shocks to their incomes, means that inequality is further aggravated and hardship is intensified.

Tourism arrivals from eleven major markets represent a significant proportion of the total international tourist arrivals to SITEs. Among these eleven markets are the world's richest seven countries, the Group of 7. The other 4 countries, namely Switzerland, Sweden, Australia and New Zealand, are among the highest per capita income countries of the world.

The eleven countries are geographically located with varying measures of distance relative to the six SITEs. These countries are diverse in their social and economic cultures, but explain more than two-thirds of the composition of international tourist arrivals in all the SITEs, except for Dominica. The capacity of the Dominican tourism industry is relatively small compared with the rest of the six SITEs.

Moreover, the relatively small magnitudes of mean percentages of tourists from a wide variety of nationalities to Dominica is the dominant feature, besides US tourists dominating the visitor profile, accounting for just below one-fifth. During the same period, in Barbados, Cyprus and Dominica, international tourist arrivals account for six of the eleven source markets. While Fiji welcomed tourists from seven of these eleven sources, Maldives and Seychelles received tourists from the most number of source markets.

The USA, UK and Germany are the dominant markets for tourists to these SITEs. Moreover, these three markets also correspond to quite substantial mean percentages across most of the SITEs. Although the USA is the world's largest and richest economy, their prominence in international tourist arrivals is notable only in the two Caribbean SITEs, namely Barbados and Dominica, followed by Fiji.

In the Indian Ocean SITEs, US tourists feature with very low mean percentages. However, UK tourists are spread more evenly among the six economies compared with US tourists. UK tourists are the most widely travelled among the eleven tourism markets, arguably because of the British colonial heritage attached to these SITEs. Generally, European tourists seem to travel to island destinations compared with US and Canadian tourists. German tourists have smaller magnitudes than their UK counterparts.

The Germans are followed by French and Italian tourists who travel more to the Indian Ocean SITEs as compared with their Mediterranean and Caribbean counterparts. Canadian, Swiss, Swedish and Japanese tourist arrivals appear among three SITEs, with varying visitor profiles. Canadians tend to travel to the Caribbean and the Pacific, Swiss and Swedish tourists are present among all the regions except the Pacific, while Japanese tourists appear in the Indian Ocean and Pacific Ocean SITEs. Australian and New Zealand tourists travel substantially to SITEs in the Pacific region, but their arrivals are relatively small among the other SITEs.

Transportation Facilites

By definition islands are pieces of land surrounded by water, and unless close enough to neighbours or mainlands to make a bridge feasible, can only be reached by boat or air. In other words, their accessibility is much more limited in most cases than that of mainland destinations, and this, in turn, makes them much more vulnerable to changes in transportation. Such changes may occur through developments in transportation technology, through political developments, through changes in economic conditions, and through changes in infrastructure. These changes, occurring singly or in combination, can have major impacts on tourism in all destinations, but particularly so in the case of island tourist destinations.

Innovation in transportation in the context of tourism can be introduced in a variety of ways. The innovations may come about as a result of technological change, as a result of economic change, as a reflection of political change, and as a result of sociocultural change. The fact that improved technology is available does not automatically mean that it will be adopted, and the length of time between appearance and adoption may reflect cultural or political conservatism and reluctance to change established patterns. Alternatively, while new technology may be available and acceptable to a society, the economic situation may be such that the innovation cannot be introduced because of cost.

In other situations, while the economic, political and cultural conditions may be ripe for the introduction of an innovation, the associated may not be, in place, this preventing the adoption of the All tend to become magnified in importance in the case of islands because of the economic and other limitations which most islands face, and the fact that they may not sufficient political influence in world markets and affairs to persuade the proprietors of innovations to introduce them to their limited markets.

It has long been the lot of islands to have to await the effects of innovations in transportation and other spheres, often for a considerable time after their introduction in the core areas of the world. In the case of tourism, the innovations may well have been introduced nonpleasure travel between core locations, such as principal cities, for any years before they are introduced to core periphery travel for tourism. The result of such a situation is the very rapid introduction of such innovations when they do take place in the tourism field, often with serious effects in the destinations because the acceptance is so rapid, and often outstrips infrastructure and legislation to control it.

It is appropriate to distinguish between innovations in transportation which are technological innovations at the time at which they are introduced, such as the railway engine, and those which are innovative because the social rid political processes have allowed them to be introduced, e.g. ferry services and air flights on religious holidays. Irrespective of the nature of the innovation, however, the effect is normally the same, namely, significant and often rapid increases in the numbers of tourists, and quite often, significant changes in the nature of tourists and their activities.

It is necessary to consider first the ways in which innovations in transportation impact upon tourism, both generally and in the case of islands in articular. Frequently, the most significant effect of innovations in transportation is to reduce the amount of time involved in travel to and from a destination. If time spent in travel is regarded as a cost, then any eduction in travel time implies a corresponding reduction in travel cost. Perhaps more important to many tourists, however, is the increase in choice of potential destinations which a reduction in travel time implies.

The advent of the railway engine and its rapid involvement in tourism represents the first transportation innovation of major significance for tourism on a large scale. The railway served to drastically reduce the amount of time needed in ravel and opened up vast areas as potential tourist destinations in all continents of the world. Most innovations have had similar effects. The automobile increased the speed of transportation by road, and the aircraft, in a series of forms, dramatically reduced he time in travel to any destination at which planes could land.

As travel to islands has frequently involved more than one form of transportation, e.g. road and boat or rail and boat, the introduction of air travel, which could not only allow faster travel but also remove the necessity of transhipment points an time spent waiting between travel, has reduced

A second effect of transportation innovation is in reducing the financial cost of travel. Almost all innovations tend to reduce the per capita cost of travel once they have been adopted on a large scale. The average cost per mile of travel for tourism, as for all forms of travel, has consistently declined in relative terms as more people travel and services can draw on a greater market, thus benefiting from economies of scale. Again, in the case of islands, where travel costs have often been disproportionately high compared to travel costs to nonisland destinations, such savings can make major differences in overall costs of an island vacation.

Third, innovations in transportation usually improve comfort and safety for passengers. By reducing travel time alone they achieve this if the travel is anything but luxurious, but in most cases safety and comfort have seen improvement with the introduction of each innovation once the period is completed. While some transportation innovations such as did not prove entirely safe and were subsequently abandoned, during even their brief spell of success the comfort of passengers improved markedly.

Travel became less of a chore and physical tourists to arrive at their destination and their homes rested after their journeys. Where the destinations, such as consider able distances from the origin regions, this became a major consideration. In the case of islands in extremely remote locations, or those situated in hazardous waters, the safety and comfort aspects of travel may have been the prime considerations of potential travellers.

Fourth, overall convenience for the traveller has normally increased. As innovations become adopted and increasingly dispersed, the level of service and its spatial pattern becomes wider, and more accessible to an increasing number of people. While massive expansion is normally followed at some time by rationalization and reduction in services, e.g. the drastic reduction in rail services in the UK in the 1960s, at least for a while the range of service is often dramatically improved.

The car has had the greatest influence in this regard, allowing travellers to begin their travels in the vehicle of choice from their home itself, often to the door at the destination. The conveyance of baggage was similarly made easier. For those islands traditionally served by vessels with limited carrying capacity or unable to carry motor vehicles, for example, significant innovations may open large new markets by improving aspects of convenience.

Finally, the innovations normally drastically improve overall accessibility, at least at global and continental scales by opening up new areas to an ever increasing market, which may reside further and further away from the destination. We now face the situation in which virtually no destination on the globe is inaccessible to tourists, because of the development and introduction of innovations in transportation . While it may be argued that travellers could always reach almost any destination during the past century or so, the cost, time, effort and logistics involved deterred many travellers from venturing far from home until well into the twentieth century.

The overall effects of the innovations are to increase the overall participation in tourism by improving the mobility of tourists. There are other effects as well. Increased participation is reflected in a variety of forms of tourism. The innovation often becomes a type of tourism itself; for example, ocean cruising is both a means of transportation and a form of tourism, and so too are flying, driving for pleasure and sailing. The increase in participation may come about also in terms of increased occasions of participation, e.g. second holidays, as fewer days have to be spent in travel, allowing more time for the actual vacation.

All of these effects of innovations apply to tourism to all destinations, but, as noted above, have particular significance in the case of island destinations because travel to islands is frequently the principal limitation on visitation and development. It should be noted as well that transportation innovations should not be viewed as a onetime occurrence only. Destinations such as islands which benefit from such improvements in technology may do so more than once.

Additional or secondary benefits may accrue from more than one innovation; for example, a destination such as Hawaii, which experienced increased visitation from the development of the steamship , could also be expected to benefit in the same way from the introduction of air services, and again from subsequent improvements in this mode of travel. The following discusses the effects of specific transportation innovations upon a selection of island destinations.

Steam Technology

The development of the railway engine is often noted as the first transportation innovation which had major effects upon tourism. Railway companies became intimately and heavily involved in the transportation of tourists and the development of tourist destinations themselves in the nineteenth century. Little of this early development of tourism and tourist places in the middle to late nineteenth century had much direct effect on islands, however, for the obvious reason that few islands were directly accessible by rail, and nor were they large enough to warrant a rail service. Those that were, e.g. New Zealand and the Isle of Man, did experience direct benefit in terms of development of tourist resources from railway development.

The innovation of the railway engine did, however, dramatically improve access to the coast, and indirectly, therefore, to offshore islands. It is clear that the spread of railway services through Britain, for example, led to coastal tourism development and the spread of tourism into many rural areas. Many ports developed as railheads, and became transhipment points for tourists wishing to visit islands, which previously had been inaccessible simply because the coastal areas themselves were too far from the main concentrations of potential tourists.

In the case of the islands off the coast of Scotland, the links between the development of railway services to coastal railheads and subsequent in creases in tourist numbers to the offshore islands is documented qualitatively if not quantitatively in many writings of the late nineteenth and early twentieth centuries. Railhead ports on the west coast of Scotland, such as Oban, Mallaig and Kyle of Lochalsh, served to bring tourists on Cook's tours and independent travellers to fleets of boats waiting to take them to such island destinations as Iona, Staffa and Skye, following in the foot steps of Johnson and Boswell, Mendelssohn, and many other literary and artistic giants.

While tourism of a limited form had existed in such island destinations before the advent of the steamship, other islands did not experience tourism beyond the occasional visitor during the sailing ship era. The Hawaiian islands, for example, had almost no intentional visitors for pleasure before the advent of steam navigation, and even by the mid-nineteenth century still experienced few tourists because of the time and distance involved. Most of the tourists who did venture to Hawaii were *en route* to Asia or the South Pacific; few were making a single destination trip to the islands.

In the case of the West Indies, however, which had developed a limited pattern of tourism or at least visitation by the end of the eighteenth century, the increase in speed and reliability introduced with the steamship ushered in the first proper tourists during the first half of the nineteenth century. Some of these visitors were the forerunners of today's cruise ship passengers, visiting several islands on a lengthy voyage, while others visited only one or two destinations.

The private steam yacht appeared in the nineteenth century and allowed the affluent elite, often the royalty and nobility, to visit many islands, which they often then acquired as personal freedoms, both in inland lakes in Canada, the USA and western Europe, and in coastal waters such as the Baltic, the Mediterranean and the Aegean.

The private steam yacht allowed consider able numbers of passengers and servants, along with large amounts of baggage, to be quickly and efficiently transported from many major capitals to holiday offshore destinations.

Car and related developments

Of all transportation innovations the car has had the largest effect upon tourism, but in the context of island destinations its direct impact has been less significant except for a few destinations, and has frequently been delayed because of the inaccessibility of many islands to large numbers of tourist driven cars. The great attraction of the car, once it became reliable, was the ability to personalize travel. Tourists could leave and return to their homes, travel by a route of their own choice to a destination, taking as long as they wished on the journeys, carrying considerable amounts of luggage and other items, and often do it all considerably cheaper than using other forms of transportation.

All that was required was road access. This, of course, was why islands did not immediately experience the full impact of the car; many of them did not have road access, meaning that the car had to be driven to a port and left there, or else be ferried across to an island port. This immediately increased the cost of travel, often added considerably to the time involved, and in some cases determined the route and timing of the trip. The key element of individual choice or flexibility was lost, even if the vehicle could be transported to the island in question. Also, at least in the early years of this century, many islands did not have reliable or extensive road net works, so a car was not a great advantage.

Air travel

In the context of island tourism the aeroplane has been the most significant transportation innovation, arguably of all time. While the ship offered increasingly reliable and faster ways of reaching island destinations, it always had the twin disadvantages to most travellers of a relatively slow speed and the necessity, except for inhabitants of port cities, of transhipment procedures, involving additional time and cost. While to some jaded twentieth century travellers the idea of leisurely and comfortable travel has its appeal, evidenced in the increasing number of people taking cruises, to those wishing to reach an island destination quickly, safely and cheaply, there is nothing to equal the aeroplane.

The impact of the aeroplane on island tourism has been felt globally, and the few places without air access are normally seeking urgently to acquire it because of the limitations its absence causes in the context of tourism. Cost and time of travel have been dramatically reduced, comfort and safety vastly improved, and an immense number of island destinations added to the potential tourist destiny.

The significant innovations in air transport for tourism came after World War II. While air travel clearly existed prior to 1939, and the wealthy and adventurous did use air travel to reach vacation destinations, particularly islands, numbers were small. Air craft could not carry large numbers of passengers and/or fly long distances. Short hops from Florida to some of the closer Caribbean islands or from the northeast USA to Bermuda, from the UK to its offshore islands and the Channel Islands, and from Spain and Portugal to the Azores and Canaries were becoming increasingly common, although expensive, before 1939.

Jumbo Jet

The last innovation to date to affect island tourism has been the appearance of the jumbo jet, carrying 300400 tourists, introduced in 1969. Several improvements have been made since then but do not represent innovations in the strict sense of the jumbo saw the final unequivocal introduction of mass tourism to many island destinations, although the seeds of this had already been sown with the introduction of the first jet aircraft a decade and half before .

Jumbo jets such as the Boeing 747 have had significant effects on those islands and island groups which have been served by such planes, although not all major island tourism destinations have had this service. Mediterranean islands in particular, such as the Balearics, the Creek islands, Malta and Cyprus, have remained served solely by smaller jets landing at relatively small airports. This reflects in part the large proportion of the tourist traffic to these islands which is charter traffic, often from regional airports in the UK and northern Europe, many of which are not capable of servicing jumbo jets, even if they could generate the traffic necessary to make jumbo services economically viable.

A similar pattern can be seen in the case of the smaller islands in the Caribbean and South Pacific, especially the out islands which do not have facilities capable of handling jumbo jets. Governments have to make sizeable investments infrastructure and services to handle the large numbers of tourists arriving simultaneously. Hotels and other services at the destination have to have the capacity to attract airlines flying jumbos and be willing to be block booked for a season. Jumbo jets brought with them all of the advantages of economy of scale in terms of operation, but all the disadvantages of large numbers of tourists arriving simultaneously and consistently in terms of the destinations.

Twostroke Engine

The introduction of the twostroke engine has had major effects upon increasing the accessibility of many smaller islands to tourism and tourists. The popularity of this power source and its widespread use in small boats, both as the only power source and as a secondary power source in sailboats, has meant that many relatively inaccessible islands, an now be easily and safer reached by potential visitors.

While the results of this improved accessibility have not had the dramatic large-scale effects of the innovations discussed above, in terms of numbers of islands affected, this innovation has probably had the greatest overall direct effect of any innovation in transportation island tourism. Countless islands in Canada, the USA and Scandinavia in particular, now have, cottages or second homes, hotels and resorts on them because of the access allowed by versions of the twostroke engine, particularly in outboard motor form.

In recent years the advent of the highspeed inflatable boat, normally powered by large outboard motors, has revolutionized nature tourism to islands. They provide fast and safe access to hitherto inaccessible islands. A variation of this is the use of such boats in the Caribbean to ferry passengers from cruise liners to 'uninhabited' ways and islands for a short visit, to provide a 'desert island' experience.

EMERGING TRENDS IN ISLAND TOURSIM

Concerned about their mixed economic performance over the last decade and the risk of marginalization in the challenging economic conditions resulting from globalisation, small island nations expect a number of steps to be taken at the Mauritius International Meeting to help them regain lost ground on trade and better achieve sustainable development. Possible solutions include retaining market access preferences, expanding information and communications technology (ICT), accelerating the use of renewable energy, making tourism sustainable and tapping the potential of island cultures.

Trade liberalization, along with erosion of trade preferences, has had severe consequences on fragile island economies. Existing preferential arrangements were dismantled under agreed rules of the World Trade Organization (WTO), affecting commodities like sugar, bananas, coffee and coconut, which small islands used to rely upon for their exports. In St. Lucia, export revenues from bananas dropped from $46.5 million in 1996 to $21.7 million in 2002.

Small island developing States (SIDS) would like to be granted a more differentiated and favourable treatment for their exports, to compensate for the high, sometimes exorbitant economic costs resulting from their remoteness and smallness, at least as an interim measure for such time as they need to diversify their economies and overcome the existing disadvantages of reliance on a few exportable products.

SIDS also wish to benefit from greater market access for their products and to gain a stronger say in multilateral trade negotiations, to compensate for their inherent disadvantages in attracting investment. In this regard, small island nations admit that they need help to enhance their capacity for trade policy analysis and trade negotiations. Many SIDS feel very strongly about this because only a few of them were part of the negotiations at the WTO when such rules were agreed.

ICTs Role in Reducing Isolation

Better and more affordable access to the Internet has become a key factor in the drive to connect island communities among themselves and to the rest of the world. Since small islands are dispersed and face limited natural resources and high transportation costs, information and communications technology (ICT) offers them great opportunities, especially in areas like e-governance, tele-medicine, e-tourism and distance learning.

But small islands still face a number of constraints, including poor telecommunications infrastructure, high cost of computers and dial-up and leased lines to the Internet, restrictive telecommunications policies and inadequacy of trained personnel. Future ICT projects would continue to largely depend on external support from donor countries and on the private sector for the islands' investment requirements in this area.

"Deliberate and prudent use of information technology will go a long way in reducing the isolation of remote islands, enabling them to deal more effectively with a host of constraints, particularly in trade, development, health, education, security and technology transfer," said the Secretary-General of the Mauritius Meeting, Anwarul Chowdhury.

Renewable Energy

Small island nations hope that investments will allow them to accelerate their transition to sustainable energy services. The need for energy remains a major source of economic vulnerability for many islands, due to their remoteness, isolation and heavy dependence on imported petroleum products, especially for local transport and electricity generated by thermal plants.

The cycles of high petroleum prices versus low commodity prices have impacted negatively on their terms of trade and on the momentum of their economies during the last 35 years. Moreover, many are dependent on biomass as their main source of household energy, which has a negative impact on ecosystems.

Over the last decade, research has produced new, commercially feasible options for energy supply, such as wind, solar and ocean tidal energy. Small island nations are keen to develop an energy agenda through these options that would be consistent with sustainable development principles and less prone to disruption from external forces. That is why they seek support to undertake a comprehensive assessment of their energy resources, to identify and develop renewable energy that is affordable and readily adaptable.

In the fields of energy and transport, a promising experiment has been initiated in Vanuatu, where coconut oil is being used, with very little modification, as an alternative to diesel in automotive engines. More than 200 minibuses already use a coconut oil/diesel mix, and a dozen use a pure coconut oil fuel. Such a system is potentially less costly, at least in the South Pacific, is environment-friendly and has the potential to stimulate employment among local coconut growers and coconut oil producers.

Making Tourism more Sustainable

Islands are a natural attraction for tourists, and this in turn generates jobs and much-needed revenue. But the tourism industry has reached such a scale that it endangers those very ecosystems and cultures that attract tourists. Tourism needs to be made more sustainable, to better benefit small island nations while protecting their culture and traditions, and to effectively conserve and manage freshwater and other natural resources.

The continuing challenge for small islands is to establish the appropriate balance between tourism development and that of other sectors of the economy, given the limits of their carrying capacity and the fact that the tourism sector places demands on other sectors of the economy. The impact of tourism on the economy of small islands depends on the proportion of funds that are retained within the local economy. Small islands seek the best ways to maximize their own economic gains, given that their tourism industries are often dominated by foreign companies.

Tourism is also sensitive to external shocks, as shown by the reduction in the numbers of tourists, and the revenues they provide to SIDS, following the terrorist attacks against New York and Bali, and during the SARS health crisis in 2003.

Cultural Industries

Small islands have come to recognize the distinctiveness of their cultural identities as a genuine economic asset. Cultural industries and initiatives are an area in which small islands have a comparative advantage and which offer a potential to diversify their economies and build their capacity to adjust to the global economy. After all, some quintessential cultural products from these islands, like songs by the late Jamaican Bob Marley and by Capeverdian Cesaria Evora, have gained universal prominence.

Trends in Marine Tourism

Marine tourism is a temporary short-term movement of people to destinations outside their normal environment and activities within a marine setting. Economic expediency however dictates that the marine tourism sector be defined more explicitly along traditional economic lines and there sector thus includes activities such as ocean and coastal water transport, hotel and restaurants, island and beach resorts, sea sports and recreation .

Statistically, there is no disaggregation of marine tourism statistics from the general or common statistical data set, and this has been the point of contention of researchers attempting to statistically quantify or enumerate the extent or the size of the marine tourism sector . The size of the sector can however, be deduced from a number of parameters such as the extent of investment and visitor statistics as well as by examining components of the marine tourism industry where research work has been done namely, the cruise industry and island tourism.

The marine tourism industry has developed over the centuries from one, which consists of 'getaway' islands for the elite of the Roman empire , to the discovery of seaside tourism in Western Europe between 1750 and 1840 , to the mass and special interest tourism of the late twentieth century.

Where marine tourism is concerned the growth of the sector is best illustrated by the significant growth of the cruise industry and island tourism. The cruise industry began on a commercial basis in 1844 when the Peninsula and Oriental Steam Navigation Company (popularly known as P & O) first organised cruises from Britain to Spain and Portugal as well as to Malaya and China . The cruise industry is now worth US 7 billion annually, and carries about 5 million passengers in North America alone. In 1998, the projected figures for the North American cruise industry stood at nearly 8 million passengers occupying 76.2 per cent of the estimated 148,540 berths-a staggering figure for an industry which started growing only twenty-five years ago. At the same time, the cruise industry is also a profitable one, averaging at about US 1,000 profit per passenger, while net sales profit to travel agents is 5 to 15 times more than that of a land-based tour package .

Besides, cruise tourism, the other significant element of marine tourism is island tourism, which in island States such as Bermuda may contribute up to 25 per cent of the Gross National Product (GNP). Increasingly, a significant portion of marine tourism activities is also associated with islands, either in the form of mass tourism activities or more specialised pursuits. And the availability of activity options, and from the point of view of tourism planners, development options will make island tourism an essential element of any country's tourism industry.

One of the regions which have benefited significantly from island tourism on a massive scale is the Caribbean, which in 1992 received over 12 million tourists from all over the world . Other regions, including Southeast Asia have also promoted island tourism as a major tourist attraction.

There are three basic reasons why marine tourism, and tourism in general will continue to grow. The socio-economic and demographic reasons have been described earlier, and the other two reasons are discussed below. Primarily, there is still a large potential for growth in the tourism sector, and the marine tourism sector as a key tourism component will naturally benefit from this growth. The projected growth of tourism receipts from US 2 trillion in 1993 to US 3 trillion by the year 2000 is a clear indication of this potential for growth .

Secondarily, the tourism sector will also benefit from improved communication and transportation technologies. These improvements will include greater access to information about tourist destination and activities, and equally importantly enhanced access to tourism locations by way of more efficient transportation. Improved transport efficiency will in turn make travelling faster, more direct and cheaper while improving access to alternative locations.

The growth of the marine tourism sector is not without its pitfalls, especially where it concerns island and special interest tourism. Both these tourism subsectors depend on the provision or existence of quality, pristine or undisturbed assets, and will decline once the quality of these assets decline .

Development of Marine Tourism in Malaysia—A Case Study

The construction of resorts, hotels, chalets and other types of accommodation dominated the growth of the marine tourism sector in Malaysia during the early to middle part of the 90s. The main source for this data, interestingly enough, was the Department of Environment, which in 1994 reported that 128 applications were received for the construction of major hotels, resorts or recreational facilities in coastal areas. These applications were for facilities with 80 or more rooms or which covers an area of 50 hectare or more, thus requiring an environmental impact assessment (EIA) to the carried out .

In monetary terms, total investments for hotel and tourism projects amounted in 1993 amounted to RM 1,620 million, up 24.8 per cent from the 1992 total of RM 1,297.6 million . Given that the majority of tourism development project for the corresponding period occur in coastal areas or on islands, it would be reasonable to assume that the bulk of these investments also went to coastal areas and islands.

While it is generally accepted that there is still room for growth in this particular sector of the marine tourism industry, it is also true that many 'prime' areas for such activities have already been developed and some areas (such as Port Dickson) risk the possibility of overcrowding and over-development. Developing less attractive or marginal areas would need large investments to make such locations attractive to tourists.

Similarly, extensive tourism activities may also contribute towards competition with other economic sectors over the use of resources. An example cited is the competition for water resources between the tourism and agricultural activities in Phuket . The above issues also point to the need to reexamine tourism facilities or accommodation development strategies with a view to promoting small to medium scale development which are less intensive and less burdensome on natural resources. With proper regulation and control small and medium scale developments could provide viable alternatives to large marine tourism facilities.

Environmental protection requirements also play a key role in determining the size and to a certain extent the viability of a tourism project. A sector, which is dependent on good environmental quality (scenic beauty, clean beaches, unpolluted waters, and undisturbed reefs) to develop and flourish, cannot afford to compromise on environmental integrity. Prevention and mitigation of environmental damage and environmental protection and conservation are now parts and parcel of good marine tourism development and management. Project proponents spend on average between RM 2,000 and RM 3 million for the preparation of Environmental Impact Assessment (EIA) reports, and much more on implementing mitigating measures recommended as a result of the assessments and in incorporating sound environmental management practices in the day-to-day running of these facilities.

Mass or common tourism activities

A Japanese International Co-operation Agency (JICA) study in 1987 reported that 60 to 70 per cent of tourists in Malaysia in 1985 visited coastal areas . The report also noted that the majority of these tourists are day-trippers who visited coastal areas, islands or beaches for picnics and basic recreational activities such as swimming. Further studies indicated that individual; families and groups made up around 60 per cent of all visitors to coastal areas .

Day-trippers while forming the majority of tourists in a marine setting, is probably the easiest to cater to, requiring only basic amenities such rubbish bins, public toilets or changing rooms and stalls to be provided near beaches.

Growth potentials

The day-trippers to coastal areas are probably the largest untapped source of revenue for the marine tourism industry. A substantial increase in revenue could be expected if these tourists were to increase their length of stay at tourist locations. Providing suitable facilities in coastal areas (comparable to the ones found in major marine tourism areas) may make coastal seashores more attractive for longer stays. The Malaysia Tourism Policy Study identifies a number of target groups for the purpose of upgrading day-trippers to over-nighters :

— Urban dwellers who should be encouraged to go on tours and beach holidays on weekends, short breaks and school holidays;

— People travelling to visit families of friends should be encouraged to spend extra days at other locations or along the way; and

— Those going on duty free shopping holidays.

New areas and opportunities

Special interest tourism is fast gaining place within the overall context of tourism and marine tourism. This is evident from the increase in sales of watersports equipment such as leisure crafts, scuba diving and sports fishing equipment from RM 20 million in 1992 to RM 30 million in 1993 ; the interest shown in the country's 38 Marine parks;

and the investments being made into the construction of marinas and other boating facilities.

Nature tourism

The 38 marine parks in Peninsular Malaysia and Labuan, the islands under the management of Sabah Parks, and a few islands yet to be protected in the South China Sea (Pulau Layang-Layang and Sipadan) are the focus of most marine-based nature tourism in Malaysia. This is evident in the increasing number of visitors to Marine Parks. However, such data are at best scanty, and may not present the true extent of visitor number and impact because of the 38 marine parks, only a few (Pulau Redang, Pulau Payar and Pulau Tioman) have visitor centres where visitor numbers are recorded.

The increase number of visitors however, also translates to increase visitor impact on fragile ecosystems in marine parks, particularly, mangroves and coral reefs. Tourism impacts (both during development and from visitors) are well documented in Malaysia and points to potential conflicts between tourism and nature conservation. These conflicts could ultimately lead to either the collapse of the tourism industry or the marine park system as noted in the editorial of the American nature conservation journal Audobon.

> "Ecotourism is big business. It can provide foreign exchange and economic reward for the preservation of natural systems and wildlife. But ecotourism also threatens to destroy the resources in which it depends. Tour boats dump garbage in the waters off Antarctica, shutterbugs harass wildlife in National Parks, hordes of us trample fragile areas. This frenzied activity threatens the viability of natural systems. At times we seem to be loving nature to death .

Yachting, boating and sailing

The purchase of leisure crafts constituted a large portion of the amount spent on watersports equipment over the past few years involving the sales of over 200 leisure crafts of various sizes and types. A large sum has also been invested in the facilities such as marinas and harbours necessary to support the growing number of yachts and boats.

The growth questions related to this element of the marine tourism industry have as much to do with its capacity to grow as it does the capacity of authorities to regulate recreational boaters. There is a general concern, that recreational boaters may not be adequately trained to handle navigational and safety aspects of boating. A concern amplified by the fact that much of the recreational boating activity is undertaken in the Strait of Malacca, one of the busiest waterways in the world. Another concern is over the pollution that may be caused by numerous leisure or pleasure crafts plying our waters. These concern could be addressed by regulatory and non-regulatory measures including enforcing of regulations, education and training as well as the development of a voluntary code of conduct for recreational boaters .

Scuba diving

Of late, there has been tremendous growth experienced by the scuba-diving industry. This growth was encouraged by increased accessibility to training, equipment as well as dive spots, and partly because of the minimal investment involved in taking-up scuba diving or catering to scuba divers as opposed to the activities described earler. On the other hand, scuba diving is probably one of the better regulated watersports activities, with an internationally governed training programmes as well as code of conduct.

The country's potential as a site for scuba diving has generally been developed in a gradual and less damaging manner. Part because of the regulatory and training process in place to ensure diver proficiency, and part because of the fact that dive resorts and facilities tend to be smaller than commonly found beach or island hotels or resorts, and cater to smaller groups of tourists. Equally importantly is the fact that the industry needs to be self regulatory to ensure the quality and integrity of the natural resources it depends upon. This is certainly an area that should be encouraged especially in increasing overall access of the activity to as many Malaysians as possible.

Sports fishing

Sports fishing is one of the latest additions to the marine-based recreation market. There is potential for development in this area, and sports fishing market may even be able to support the establishment of small to medium scale industries to support the need of anglers in areas such as the production of fishing equipment, provision of tackles and baits and small crafts construction.

In a cursory examination of sports fishing in Malaysia , it was noted that the infrastructure needed to support the substantial growth of the sector is still lacking. The study also recommended a number of steps, which should be taken before sports fishing in Malaysia, could be developed in a 'big' way. These steps include assessing and describing the current status of sports fishing in Malaysia; and putting in place the necessary control mechanisms at Federal or State Government levels.

Despite these limitations, it is observable that the sports fishing industry is growing judging from the fishing tours being organised to fishing spots in the South China Sea, and the popularity of the angling tournaments being organised locally.

Negative Impacts of Tourism

While tourism has undoubtedly brought substantial rewards to small isiands, it has often been accompanied by negative economic consequences that are associated with domination by multinational companies, low levels of local involvement and high leakage rates of foreign exchange earnings. Islands that have built up major tourism industries may also have experienced considerable social and environmental problems. Undesirable socio cultural spillovers include casino gambling, cheap commercialization of folklore and historical attractions, rising levels of crime and the erosion of local social values in tandem with the admiration of foreign lifestyles.

The environmental problems of tourism usually relate to the concentration of tourism activity on coast lands and to the absence of a rigorous planning system. This has resulted in haphazard development, urbanization of the coast, dumping of building waste and the loss of agricultural land and vegetation. Another fundamental concern relates to the difficulty in predicting future patterns of arrivals, which in turn has created problems of matching the supply of accommodation and facilities to flows of visitors. Moreover, such problems are dynamic and unstable and are compounded in many islands by an over-reliance on one or two major sources of visitors.

In response to these challenges, island tourism planners are now seeking to diversify away from the attractions of 'sun, sea and sand', which are typical of mass tourism, into special activity holidays and business travel characterized by higher spending patterns and niche segments of the market, such as the elderly who are more likely to visit outside the summer season. Moreover, a number of islands have sought to place limits on new development, protect areas of outstanding national beauty and rehabilitate older resorts in an effort to create better conditions for sustainable tourism in the longer term.

2

Island Tourism in India

Tourism has major potential for India at our stage of transformation and development. It puts equal value on our untouched natural resources and culture. It celebrates our birthright as a nation and has huge potential for speeding up economic empowerment and transformation.

As India opened her gates towards a more open economy, tourism has evolved into a highly structured industry with the potential to earn immense revenues. Being in the services industry, it offers high value-added markets with considerable returns on investments.

Tourism has a multiplier effect on people involved in catering, transportation, shops, travel agencies, proprietors of tourist business and entrepreneurs supporting the tourism industry. This becomes a real boon in places where industry activity is low.

In India Island tourism in concentrated on two of its Union territories: Lakshadweep and Andaman and Nicobars. They are blessed with good climate and biodiversity. Annually thousands of tourists are arriving to these small islands and they play an important role in the development of tourism industry in India. This chapter discusses the tourism opportunities of these tiny landscapes.

Toursim in Lakshadweep Islands

The charm of the Lakshadweep Islands is their remote pristine splendour; they attract no merrymakers to their shores. Or, perhaps, it is the beauty of the islands, densely covered with coconut palms, and threaded by an unbroken line of creamy sand, each island serenely set in a sea whose waters range from palest aquamarine and turquoise to deepest sapphire and lapis lazuli. Yet again, it may be that their unique charm lies in the fact that each island, a tiny principality in itself, has existed from time immemorial, with little influence from the outside world.

Whatever the reason for Lakshadweep's magic, one fact is certain - it is the island paradise of your dreams. There is silence here, unbroken but for the cry of a seabird, or the sound of the waves lapping the shores. The water is so pristine one can see the myriad different fish among the corals. While snorkelling or deep sea diving, the waters come alive with amazing clarity and colour.

Tucked away in the Arabian Sea, off the coast of mainline India, the islands of Lakshadweep retain the culture and ethos of scant few places, still untouched by the madding crowd and the hurried pace of progress.

Not much is known of the early history of Lakshadweep. However, enough evidence exists to piece together a history of the islands from the 7th century. The population was converted to Islam under the influence of Hazrat Ubaidullah who set off from Mecca after Prophet Mohammed appeared to him in a dream, commanding him to leave for distant shores to propagate Islam. There was a shipwreck and after drifting on a plank of wood, he reached the island of Amini where his mission met with fierce opposition.

After much struggle he was successful in achieving his aim and now the people of Lakshadweep follow Islam. Traces of the old culture still linger. Despite the influence of Islam, a caste system still prevails based on occupation-landowners, sailors and cultivators. Although Madrassas in all the islands impart religious instruction to school going children, many individuals bear two names.

The Lakshadweep archipelago consists of 12 atolls, rich in guano, deposited by centuries of bird droppings, 3 reefs and 5 submerged banks. There are 10 inhabited and 17 uninhabited islands located between 8 ° - 12 °13' North latitude and 71 ° -74 ° East longitude, 220 to 440 km west of the Kerala coast, in the Arabian sea. Minicoy, the southernmost island is 183 km from Kalpeni, its nearest neighbour. Androth, the eastern most island is nearest to the mainland. The islands are a northern extension of the Maldives chain and are formed of coral rocks surrounded by semi-circular lagoons. Most islands are just 4-5 m above sea level.

Climatic conditions are similar to that of Kerala coast. Average rainfall is 1600 mm a year with a major share received from the southwest monsoon. They experience a tropical climate with temperature ranging from 25 degrees C to 35 degrees C and humidity ranging from 70 -76 per cent for most of the year. March to May is the hottest period of the year.

Ethnically the people of the islands are similar to the population of Kerala. Even the language is the same except in Minicoy where Mahl is spoken. They follow conservative customs and traditions but are liberal in approach. The people are friendly and honest and there is an absence of crime. Testimony to this is the profusion of gold ornaments worn by the women. Young children are spotted wandering alone wearing chunky jewellery. 93% of the population is indigenous. According to the 1991 census, the population was 51,707.

History comes alive in folk ballads that women chant during household chores. Memories of the past - the arrival of Hazrat Ubaidulla in Lakshadweep, the plunder of the islands by the Portuguese, are kept alive by the balladeer. The men have spirited folk dances. Women are modest and dress colourfully. In Minicoy there is a profusion of colour, on houses, furniture and boats. There are many seamen from Minicoy on merchant ships all over the world.

Lakshadweep has a simple economy but it is not a closed one. Wealth is still assessed by the number of coconut trees one owns. Coconut is cultivated in every available space. The annual yield of nuts is approximately 26.5 million. The fishing industry is the other major source of income. The annual fish landing crossed the level of 10,000 MTs a few years ago. There are subsidiary industries based on coconut and fishery.

Boat building was once an important skill that may soon be lost with the advent of motorized boats. Majestic wooden boats anchored along the shore stand in silent testimony to the past. Boats were built differently, according to function and every island has a slight variation in design. While sighting a boat one could deduce the island it came from.

Tourism Opportunities

Tourism in these islands is restricted to minimise damage to the environment. As a tourist one can indulge in adventure sports such as scuba and snorkelling or simply commune with nature in virtual solitude on a holiday that will be different from any other you've even enjoyed. There are Govt. organised package tours of the islands where one can stay on board ship during the travel. Only four islands have opened for domestic tourism and one, Bangaram, has been opened to International Tourism.

Kavaratti

The administrative capital, Kavaratti is the most developed with the highest proportion of non-islanders residing. 52 mosques are spread all over, the most beautiful being the Ujra mosque. A well at this mosque is believed to contain water with curative powers. The mosque has an ornately carved ceiling, carved from a piece of driftwood. Kavaratti also has an aquarium displaying several species of fish. There are glass-bottomed boats for viewing marine life and an array of remarkable coral formations that provides a background to the lagoon. Water Sports like kayaking canoeing and snorkelling are available for tourists.

Kalpeni

Kalpeni has three uninhabited satellite islands, each surrounded by an immense lagoon of spectacular beauty. Sunlight on the water causes it to sparkle and flash like a million aquamarines. Koomel, the gently curving bay where the tourist facilities are located, directly overlooks Pitti and Thilakkam, two of the islands. Here you can swim, reef walk, snorkel or use water sports equipment like kayaks and sail boats. Tourist facilities have been augmented and tourists can stay in privately managed huts. The lagoon is especially rich in coral life.

Kadmat

A particularly fine lagoon, of even depth and an endless shoreline, perfect for swimming, makes Kadmat a haven of solitude. The tourist huts are situated away from the inhabited side of the island, with only the splash of the waves to break the silence. During the day, when the beat of the overhead sun becomes too strong, the feathery network of coconut palms provides a canopy through which light dimly filters green and cool. It is the only island with lagoons on both the eastern and western sides. A Water Sports Institute has been set up. Accommodation consists of AC and non-AC tourist huts aesthetically situated amidst coconut palm groves close to beach. The island is becoming increasingly popular with honeymooners. A Scuba Diving Centre has been set up and wonderful dives are possible.

Minicoy

Furthest from Kavaratti island, 200 km. away to the south and nearer to the Maldives, Minicoy displays a lighthouse built by the British in 1885. Visitors are allowed to the very top. The lagoon is one of the largest in Lakshadweep. The green of coconut trees and the mirror-like surface of an inland lake as it nestles in one corner of the island provide an immensely beautiful seascape. Minicoy possesses a culture very different from the other islands - in dress, language and food. There is a cluster of 10 villages, called Athiris, each presided over by a Moopan. A walk through the winding lanes of the villages can be culturally rewarding. Minicoy is renowned for its dance tradition: the lava dance is performed on festive occasions. There is a Tuna canning factory. Tourists can stay in privately managed cottages.

Agatti

This island is best known because of the only airport which is situated here. This island has become the gateway to Lakshadweep and has a beautiful lagoon. A 20 bed tourist complex has been set up here.

Bangaram

The island is open to foreign tourists and has an exotic tourist resort. Tear-drop shaped, it is encircled by a halo of creamy sand. Like the other islands luxuriant plantations of coconut provide coolness even during the hottest part of the day. There are three uninhabited islands in the same atoll consisting of Tinnakara, Parali-I, Parali-II. These are easily accessible by outboarding, sailing rowing and, for the adventurous, by kayaking or wind-surfing. All the islands share the same lagoon, an enormous bowl of turquoise blue. At twilight, the setting sun, a ball of crimson in a flaming sky, casts its reflection on the water and with the coconut palms as a black silhouette, Bangaram is simply alluring.

The warm, clear, deep waters of the Indian Ocean are an irresistible invitation to the scuba diving fraternity. The exquisite coral formations include black coral formations. There is a large variety of coral fish-angel, clown, butterfly, surgeon, groupers, turtles, not to mention the abundance of adrenaline generating sharks, manta rays, sting rays and moray eels. Diving here is an addictive experience, and any diver will be proud to display the stamp of dives at Bangaram. The philosophy is to preserve marine life in its original state of purity, where coral and the shell and marine life are left undisturbed. The Bangaram Island Resort is fast becoming a "must do" among the island hoppers of the world

Andaman & Nicobar Islands

A fantasy world of silver sands, clear blue seas, coral reefs, swaying palms, tropical forests, volcanic mountains and a gently undulating landscape. One of the world's last outposts of virgin rain forest islands, the Andaman &

Nicobar Islands are a string of 300 odd islands in the Bay Of Bengal. Remote, not easily accessible, it was preserved the way it had evolved, still inhabited by tribes considered to be the oldest living communities in the world.

A fantasy world of silver sands, clear blue seas, coral reefs, swaying palms, tropical forests, volcanic mountains and a gently undulating landscape. Boasting of an idyllic landscape and immense natural attractions, it is one of the popular tourist destinations in the country.

Located between the Indian mainland and the long Burma (Myanmar) coast up to Sumatra, these coral islands with a unique ecology of its own, were till recently inhabited by tribals. The islands were annexed by the British in the 19th century and used as a penal colony for Indian freedom fighters. During World War II, the Japanese occupied the islands and created their own record of cruelty. The local tribes took up guerrilla activities against the Japanese. After India gained independence in 1947, the islands were incorporated into the Indian Union. Port Blair is the administrative headquarters of islands. The Andaman and Nicobar Islands comes under the rule of the central Government of India.

The main islands in the Andamans are Land Fall Island, Middle Andaman, South Andaman, Port Blair and Little Andaman. Nicobar, lying to the south, comprises of Car Nicobar, Great Nicobar, Chowra, Teresa, Nancowrie, Katchal and Little Nicobar. The two groups of islands, Andaman and Nicobar, are separated by a deep ten degree channel. 12 of the islands, particularly Car Nicobar in the north, are inhabited, while Great Nicobar, the largest and southernmost island in the group, is virtually uninhabited. The main aboriginal group in the Andamans are the Onges, who live on Little Andaman. The Nicobarese, the largest group, seem to be of mixed Burmese, Malay, Mon and Shan origin. They are a friendly and cheerful lot, who do not accept money and prefer the barter system.

The capital of this Union Territory is Port Blair, on the Andaman Islands, which is the landing and departure point for boat excursions in the Andamans and an ideal base for touring the archipelago of 321 islands. The island has been named after Lt. Reginald Blair, who conducted a survey of the area, in 1789. One of the fascinating features of the land that can be seen throughout the islands, is that of houses built on poles. The island also houses all the administrative and government buildings and people from all parts of the world live here, thus, giving it a rather cosmopolitan look.

The main aboriginal group in the Andamans are the Onges, who live on Little Andaman. Onges, like other Andamanese tribes, are of Negrito origin. They are food-gatherers who hunt, fish and collect honey, and are the only tribe on the islands, who freely accept contact with the outside world. In the Nicobars, the only aboriginals are the Shompens, who are averse to any contact with the outside world. The Nicobarese, the largest group, seem to be of mixed Burmese, Malay, Mon and Shan origin. They are a friendly and cheerful lot, who do not accept money and prefer the barter system. Communing with the dead is one of the many intriguing rituals practiced in Nicobar.

Deserted beaches, exquisite coral life and clear waters offer delightful opportunities for snorkeling and diving. Often referred to as the perfect tropical paradise, the Andaman and Nicobar islands form the peaks of a vast submerged mountain range that extends between Myanmar and Sumatra. This colony of 300 islands stretch over 500 miles in the Bay of Bengal. Situated east of the Indian mainland between the 6th and 14th parallel of north latitude and between 92 degree and 94 degree of east longitude, the islands run on Indian time so the sun rises at 4 am and darkness falls soon after 5 pm.

The islands are in two groups: the Andamans and the Nicobar, with a ten-degree channel separating the two. The bulk of the 239 Andaman Islands comprise of North, Middle and South Andamans, which along with Baratang and Rut-Land forms one landmass known as the Great Andamans.

The Nicobar Islands are located 50 km south of Little Andaman. 13 of the 19 Nicobar Islands are inhabited by about 12,000 aboriginal tribesmen most of whom live on Car Nicobar, the northern most of the archipelago. Port Blair, the capital of the Andaman and Nicobar Islands is 780 miles from Calcutta, 749 miles from Chennai and120 miles from Cape Negrais in Myanmar.

The bulk of the 239 Andaman Islands comprise of North, Middle and South Andamans, which along with Baratang and Rut-Land forms one landmass known as the Great Andamans. The islands have a number of harbours notably Port Blair in the south, Elphinstone and Bonington in the middle, Port Cornwallis in the north and the landlocked Nancowry Harbour between the islands of Kamotra and Nancowry. The population density is 34 people per sq. km and the literacy rate is 74 %. The main languages are Hindi, Bengali, Tamil, Malyalam and Telugu.

Over 90% of the territory is under forest cover which forms the major source of income. About 50 % of the forest has been set aside as Tribal Reserves, National Parks and Wildlife Sanctuaries. Rich luxuriant mangroves occupy nearly 11.5 % of the territory. More then 150 plant and animal species are rife. Coconut, which grows in abundance, is the main item of trade and diet of the locals.

Deserted beaches, exquisite coral life and clear waters offer delightful opportunities for snorkeling and diving.

The main aboriginal group in the Andamans are the Onges, who live on Little Andaman. Onges, like other Andamanese tribes, are of Negrito origin. They are food-gatherers who hunt, fish and collect honey, and are the only tribe on the islands, who freely accept contact with the outside world. In the Nicobars, the only aboriginals are the Shompens, who are averse to any contact with the outside world. The Nicobarese, the largest group, seem to be of mixed Burmese, Malay, Mon and Shan origin. They are a friendly and cheerful lot, who do not accept money and prefer the barter system. Communing with the dead is one of the many intriguing rituals practiced in Nicobar.

The Cellular Jail which housed freedom fighters and political activists who were sentenced to two decades of imprisonment on these islands came to be known as Kala Pani or Black Water.

The Roman geographer Ptolemy first referred to the Andaman and Nicobar Islands as the island of cannibals, in the second century AD. Chinese Buddhist monk, Xuan Zang in the seventh century and Arabian travellers in the ninth, spoke of the inhabitants as fierce and cannibalistic. Marco Polo's description of the islanders in the 13th century was similar.

Contrary to the above descriptions, accounts of the ferocity of the Andamanese seem to be propagated by Malay pirates who held sway over the surrounding seas and needed to keep looters well away from trade ships that passed between India, China and the Far East.

In the seventeenth century the islands witnessed Maratha Rule. Several futile attempts to convert the

Nicobarese to Christianity were made by the French, Dutch and Danish, in the 17th and 18th centuries, when plans were abandoned in the face of repugnant diseases and a severe lack of food and water. Trading companies met with a more treacherous fate at the hands of the Nicobarese with their ships captured and their crew murdered.

Chinese Buddhist monk, Xuan Zang in the seventh century and Arabian travellers in the ninth, spoke of the inhabitants as fierce and cannibalistic. Regular prisoners and political activists of the Mutiny of 1857 were made to clear land and build their own prison. Most lost their lives while trying to escape, were hung or attacked by the Andamanese who objected to deforestation.

Port Blair became a penal colony at the end of the nineteenth century. The Cellular Jail built over a period of 18 years from 1890 to 1908 housed thieves and smugglers but later, on the lines of Sumatra, Singapore and Penang, freedom fighters and political activists were sentenced to two decades of imprisonment on these islands, which came to be known as Kala Pani or Black Water. Made up of hundreds of tiny solitary cells it was used to confine political prisoners until 1945. During World War II the islands were occupied by the Japanese, who tortured and murdered hundreds, suspected of collaborating with the British. British forces moved back in 1945 and abolished the penal settlement.

The Andaman and Nicobar Islands were constituted into a Union Territory of the Indian Union in November 1956. Since then a lot of effort has gone into the development of the Andaman Islands as a tourist resort. More woodland has been cleared and new industries established. But it has had an adverse effect on the needs and rights of the tribal settlers. A majority of the population of the Andamans has migrated from Bangladesh and Bengal. Administrators are appointed from Delhi on a two-year posting and no significant development has taken place in the last couple of years. The Indian Navy patrols the islands and the sea around to keep it free from gunners and drug smugglers.

The Andaman Islanders were foragers, subsisting on whatever they could hunt, fish, or collect.

The origin of the indigenous population of the Andaman and Nicobar Islands is shrouded in mystery. It is believed that Negrito communities may have migrated here from the east and north when the islands were connected to Burma, or the sea was sufficiently shallow to allow transport by canoe. Their survival has been under constant threat ever since Western traders and colonizers introduced disease, indulged in widespread deforestation and brought about rapid cultural disintegration of the population. It is estimated that of the 5000 aborigines in 1858 less than 700 inhabitants remained by 1950 in both the Great and Little Andaman groups.

Divided into 12 or 13 'tribes' or tribal units on the basis of linguistic and cultural differences, the Andaman Islanders are clustered into two major groups; a 10-tribe group in the Great Andamnas and 2 or 3 tribes in the Little Andamans.

On the Nicobar Islands, the Mongoloid Nicobarese claiming descent from a Burmese prince have integrated with recent settlers and while they continue to live in small communities of grass huts raised on stilts, have adopted modern agricultural methods, raising pigs rather than hunting. Less than 200 of the still unaccustomed Shompen of Great Nicobar live on the coast and barter in honey, cane and nuts with the Nicobarese in isolated pockets further inland.

The Shompen of Great Nicobar live on the coast and barter in honey, cane and nuts with the Nicobarese in isolated pockets further inland. Most of Great Andamanese died of diseases contracted from western settlers and the trickle who remain are settled today on Strait Island, north of South Andaman.

The Jarawas who were originally located on the present site of Port Blair, now live on the western coasts of Middle and South Andaman, hemmed in by the Andaman Trunk Road, which since the 1970s has cut them off from hunting grounds and fresh water supplies. Nevertheless, possessive about their land, they remain unwilling to mix and contact with settlers is limited to gift-exchange at each full moon, a time of celebration.

The Onges were once used by the Chinese and Japanese to dive for valuable shells in exchange for alcohol and opium. Today the largest tribe on the Andaman Islands they live on Little Andaman and Rutland Island in communal shelters (bera) and construct temporary thatched huts (korale). Unlike other tribes, the Onges do not practice tattooing, but they paint their bodies with white clay and ochre, and the women smear themselves with yellow dye from orchids.

The most evasive tribe of all, the Sentinelese, live on North Sentinel Island west of South Andaman. In 1991, the local administration established some contact with them by way of gifts left on the beaches every month. on Strait Island, north of South Andaman. The amazing racial and cultural mix of the present day settlers correctly describes the Andamans as mini India.

The Andaman Islanders were foragers, subsisting on whatever they could hunt, fish, or collect. The Andaman communities, divided into eramtaga (jungle-dwellers), and ar-yuato (coast dwellers) subsist on fish, turtles, turtle eggs, pigs, fruits, honey and roots. Bows and arrows were used for both hunting and fishing. Harpoon fishing and hunting with dogs appear to have been later introductions. Reef collection was done with nets. Males were primarily hunters and fishers but also engaged in secondary collection activities. Females were primarily collectors of vegetable products, reef fauna and small animals. The Andaman Islanders' animal foods included pig, civet cat, lizards, rats, snakes, insects, birds, turtles, fish, mollusks and crustaceans. The bulk of their diet, however, came from fruits, roots, seeds and other plant products. Seasonal feasts of wild honey are also noted in literature.

Local groups, or bands, consisted of about 20-50 members; each group associated with a traditional resource territory, throughout which it moved during the year. Local groups could usually obtain permission to forage in neighboring territories. There were no tribal chiefs and leadership on the local level was based on respect for the advice of older and more talented members of the community. Disputes were amicably settled by interested parties.

The typical household seems to have been the monogamous nuclear family. Partners were frequently found in other groups or tribes and post marital residence patterns were flexible. Divorce was rare, especially after the birth of the first child. Adoption was a common feature of Andaman society. Both males and females underwent puberty rites. Shamans were thought to have special powers for curing, sorcery and dream interpretation and was achievable by either males or females, but such achievement depended on the acceptance by the group of the individual's claim to special powers. The cosmology of the Andaman

Islanders contained a variety of animistic spirits and spirits of the dead.

Daily ritual dances central to communal life were held on land enclosed by huts. Intergroup contacts were generally peaceful; their dwellers getting together at times of abundance. The present day settlers comprise people of all faiths - Hindus, Muslims, Christians, Sikhs who speak languages like Hindi, Bengali, Malayalam, Tamil, Telugu, Punjabi. They live together in complete harmony. Inter-religion and inter-regional marriages are common. The amazing racial and cultural mix correctly describes the Andamans as mini India.

The best time to visit these tropical islands is between mid November and April. The climate remains tropical throughout the year with temperatures varying between 24°C and 35°C. Due to the incessant sea breeze; Andamans has very humid weather. The southwest monsoon touches the Indian soil first in the Andamans and then proceeds towards the mainland. From mid-May to October, heavy rains flush the islands, often bringing violent cyclones that leave the west coast beaches strewn with fallen trees. In November and December less severe rains arrive with the northeast monsoon. The best time to visit these islands is between mid November and April.

The major industries include PVC conduit pipes and fittings, paints and varnishes, fibre glass, soft drinks and beverages and steel furniture.

Luxurious rainforests make the Andamans a gold mine for timber. Tropical fruits are found on the hilly parts of the islands in abundance, while the potential for fishery offers industrial possibilities. Paddy is the main cash crop here, while coconut and arecanut are the main cash crops of the Nicobar islands. Field crops, namely pulses, oilseeds and vegetables and spices like pepper, cloves, nutmeg and cinnamon are also cultivated. Rubber, red oil, palm and cashew are grown on a limited scale on these islands. The major industries in the region include PVC conduit pipes and fittings, paints and varnishes, fibre glass, soft drinks and beverages and steel furniture.

The islands are covered by thick green jungles, dotted with sandy beaches on the fringes and inhabited by many unique species of birds The real attraction for the tourist lies in the crystal clear seas that harbour some of the world's richest and unspoilt marine reserves. This island is splendid with its golden, crescent - shaped beaches, mangrove forests, rich marine life, exotic flora and fauna. Filled with dazzling fish and kaleidoscopic corals, and roamed by schools of dolphins and sharks, the waters are perfect for snorkelling and scuba diving.

Tourism Oppportunites

From a tourist point these islands have immense potential. The clear waters and white sandy beaches make Andamans a perfect tropical paradise. The Andamans are surrounded by shallow coral reefs and a clear sea. It is an ideal location for a relaxed holiday. But there are many out of bound and protected areas. Indians have more freedom to explore the islands than foreigners who are not allowed to enter any of the Nicobar islands.

The Andamans have immense potential but they are not being tapped properly. The development has been insignificant but the population has increased alarmingly. There has been migration of the Tamils who were expelled from Sri Lanka. This tropical paradise though green at present will not remain the same for long due to the rapid clearing of forests in the name of development. The natural teak forests are being cleared for the rubber plantation. On the whole, the islands are good for tourism but not for long duration of stay.

The Cellular Jail is Port Blair's only firm reminder of its gloomy past. The sturdy brick Cellular Jail or Kala Pani overlooks the sea from a small rise in the northeast of town.

Located on the east coast of South Andaman, Port Blair, the capital of Andaman and Nicobar Islands, is a remote harbour. With just a cluster of tin-roofed houses, shops, restaurants and offices, it is a tourist destination less by choice and more because of necessity. It is the arrival point for the islands, and the only place with a bank, tourist offices and hotels.

Mineral water and other essentials are available here, only marginally more expensive than the mainland. Power, water and sewerage systems are beginning to show signs of being over-stretched and there are frequent breakdowns. Port Blair offers a variety of sea food delicacies, besides Indian, Chinese, Continental, and Burmese cuisine.

Cellular Jail or Kala Pani

Port Blair's only firm reminder of its gloomy past, the sturdy brick Cellular Jail or Kala Pani overlooks the sea from a small rise in the northeast of town. Seven wings originally radiated from the central tower out of which only three remain, the rest being destroyed by the Japanese.

Built over a period of eighteen years at the start of the 20th century by the British, its dingy solitary cells were quite different and far worse than the dormitories in other prison blocks erected earlier. The prisoners endured extremely grim conditions in the dirty and ill-ventilated cells where drinking water was limited to two glasses per day and the convicts were expected to wash in the rain as they worked, clearing forests and building prison quarters. Food was stored in vats where the rice and pulses became infested with worms; more than half the prison population died long before their twenty years' detention was up. Frequent executions took place in full view of the cells, at the gallows that still stand in squat wooden shelters in the courtyards.

Corbyn's Cove, a 7 km walk away, is the nearest beach to Port Blair. The nearby Snake Island is surrounded by coral reefs. Currents in the water here are pretty strong and swimming can be dangerous. The sound and light show (in English on Wed, Sat & Sun 7.15pm; in Hindi daily at 6pm; except for the rainy season) outlines the history of the prison, and a small museum by the entrance gate (open at the same hours as the prison) exhibits lists of convicts, photographs and grim torture devices.

Samudrika Marine Museum

Run by the Indian Navy, the marine museum has tanks brimming with exotic fish and coral from the islands' reefs. The five sections of this unique museum display history and geography of the Andaman & Nicobar islands. Displays include miniature models of islands, pictures of tribals and their life-style and archaeology.

Aquarium

This aquarium cum museum has a collection of some 350 species of marine animals found in the Andaman Sea.

Anthropological Museum

On MG Road in the west of town, the anthropological museum illustrates the lives of the aboriginal tribes with miniature models of the tools used by them, their dresses and photographs of their life style. Above the museum is a well stocked library where you can look up books.

Mini Zoo and Forest Museum

The small zoo has 200 species of animals and birds which include the Nicobar Pigeon, the Andaman Pigand and the rare agile luminous-green Andaman gekko. A salt-water crocodile farm that breeds and releases crocodiles into the coastal mangrove swamps is a part of the zoo. Near the zoo is the museum maintained and run by the forest department. This unusual museum displays local types of wood used in the timber industry such as padauk which has both light and dark colours present in the same tree, rosewood and marble wood. Lumbering methods are clearly explained here.

Chatham Sawmill

5 km North-west of Aberdeen Bazaar, on the peninsula that marks the northernmost edge of Port Blair, is the British built Chatham sawmill one of the oldest and largest timber processing plants on Indian territory. The seasoning of beautiful and rare woods taken from various islands is a sad testimony to continuing felling; photography is prohibited. Most of the timber goes from here to the mainland.

Water Sports Complex

Very close to the Fisheries Museum, is the water sports complex where you can rent rowboats, wind surfing equipment, sailing dinghies and snorkels. Water skiing is also available.

Chiriya Tapu, 30 Km from Port Blair is at the southern tip of South Andaman. A tiny fishing village it has beautiful mangroves, shell-strewn beaches, sharp rocks and vast coral reefs. South of the island is a beach well known for snorkelling.

Mt Harriet

Mount Harriet at 365 m is one of the highest points in South Andaman. A natural trail leads to the summit. Permission to climb the nature trails that weave through dense forest must be obtained from the Chief Wildlife Warden in Haddo.Open to tourists during the day, permission of the warden at Port Blair has to be taken to stay overnight in the forest rest house. Towards the north is the Mt Harriet National Park where one can watch elephants being trained to carry logs. One can take a ferry service or taxi from the Chatnam wharf to Bamboo flat. The summit , 7 km from here is an enjoyable walk but the route is devoid of drinking water. Taxis and jeeps are also available.

Madhuban

Ferries from Phoenix Bay Jetty to Bamboo Flat and a short bus ride gets you to Madhuban a felling area where elephants work alongside men. Private vehicles can be ferried from Chafham jetty to Bamboo Flat, which saves a long drive over poor roads on the route from Port Blair.

Ross Island

Ross Island was the administrative headquarters of the British during World War II. Formerly known as Paris of the East, this place now lies in ruins. Its manicured lawns adorned with umbrellas and shades and the majestic ballrooms were destroyed in an earthquake in 1941. Daily services were held at the Church but now forest and under growth has over-run the place which is in ruins and has a somewhat haunting air of poignancy. The small museum near the jetty presents a picture of the bygone era. The island is under Naval control and it is mandatory to sign the visitor's guest book on arrival. Ferries from Phoenix Bay take 20 minutes for the ride to Ross Island.

Corbyn's Cove

The nearest beach to Port Blair, it is a pleasant 7 km walk. The nearby Snake Island is surrounded by coral reefs. Currents in the water here are pretty strong and swimming can be dangerous.

Sippighat Farm

Located 15 km from Port Blair en route to Wandoor, this Government owned farm is used for research in various kinds of agricultural products. Research predominantly in spices has developed new varieties of cinnamon, pepper, nutmeg and cloves.

Wandoor

This stunningly beautiful group of 15 islands forms part of the 280 sq kms Mahatma Gandhi Marine National Park. There are a number of good beaches on Wandoor but watch for the strong currents. Do not venture on the corals as they might get damaged. Many coral reefs have already been damaged due to over enthusiastic visitors.

Part of the Wandoor national park, Red Skin and Jolly Buoy islands boast a stunning array of over 50 varieties of coral and fish. Daily boat trips are organised to these uninhabited islands (departures from Wandoor jetty, daily except Mon, 10am). Food and drink are usually provided on the organized tours, which also provide transport from Port Blair to Wandoor. Although the trips give less than three hours to explore the fabulous reefs, they are still worthwhile.

Chiriya Tapu

At the southern tip of South Andaman, an hour's drive from Port Blair, is Chiriya Tapu or Bird Island; a tiny fishing village with mangroves, shell-strewn beaches, sharp rocks and vast coral reefs. South pf the island is a beach well known for snorkelling.

Cinque Island

South of Chirya Tapu, the uninhabited Cinque Island are surrounded by some of the finest coral reefs which can be seen a few hundred metres into the sea. Permission from the Forest Department is required to visit these islands and a night visit is rarely granted. It takes two and a half hours to get here by boat from Chiriya Tapu and three and a half hours from Wandoor. Ferries between Phoenix Bay and the island run only once a week (3hr).

Diglipur

It is the northernmost point of the Andaman chain. 9 km inland from its harbour at Arial Bay is a bazaar. One can swim at a small beach beside the mangrove swamps near a sawmill. A sandy beach, 11 km further on at Kalipur is connected by bus. Permission to make the three- to four-hour climb up the thickly forested Saddle Peak must be obtained from the Range Officer at Arial Bay. The nearby Austin Islands are also worth a visit.

Long Island

The several sandy beaches on this island, which is off the south east coast of Middle Andaman are an idyllic camping site. It has a forest rest house and a PWD rest house. On Wednesdays and Saturdays ferries from Port Blair and Havelock stop here on their way to Rangat.

Neil Island

Predominantly inhabited by post-partition Bengali settlers, the Neil Islands offer good beaches for snorkelling. Some of the corals here have been damaged due to extensive fishing. The numbered beaches are popular for their hammocks under shady trees. The largest of Neil's wide and deserted beaches is at Sitapur, on the east coast.

Viper Islands

The islands got its name from a ship The Viper, which was wrecked nearby. Gallows, whipping posts and crumbling walls of the gallows remind one of the days of the Raj. Convicts were made to stay for a month to deter them from breaking prison discipline. Harbour cruises from Port Blair (daily 3-5pm; Rs20) include a short stop on Viper Island.

Middle Andamans

The Grand trunk Road links Port Blair to the Middle Andamans. Public transport has armed guards to ward off any attacks from the native Jarawa tribes who are very hostile to visitors. Independent travelling in this area is discouraged even though the island is open to the tourists and accommodation & other facilities have been provided. Tourists can also visit Rangat and Mayabunder islands.

Little Andamans

Home to the Onge tribals, who are confined to the south of the island, these reserves are out of bound areas. The waves make this place good for swimming. There is police station where one has to register his arrival. The main beach of Little Andamans is at Butler Bay, which is also a camping ground.

Scuba Diving in the Andaman Islands

Andamans are Coral islands with white sand beaches and surrounded by pristine beauty of Nature. The seas around the Andaman and Nicobar Islands are some of the world's finest, relatively unexplored, unspoiled and multi-hued. Many species of fish and coral are unique to the area and fascinating life systems exist in ash beds and cooled lava around the eastern volcanic island of Barren. One can start by snorkelling; most hotels supply masks and snorkels. However, the only way to get really close, and venture out into deeper waters, is to scuba dive. The experience of weaving in and out of coral beds, coming eye to eye with fish or swimming with dolphins and barracudas is unforgettable, and at prices that are among the lowest in the world, it's an opportunity not to be missed.

The dive centers The Samudra, Port Blair Underwater and Andamans Adventure Sports and the recently established Andaman and Nicobar Scuba Diving Society run by Mr Chowdhary have almost similar rates. These centers have good equipment and the guides are well experienced. It's not uncommon to come across schools of sharks, which rarely turn hostile, but one thing to watch out for and avoid is the black-and-white sea snake. Though the snakes seldom attack - and, since their fangs are at the back of their mouths, would find it difficult to get a grip on any human - their bite is more deadly than that of the cobra.

It's essential to respect the environment when diving and snorkelling. Increased tourism inevitably puts pressure on the delicate marine eco-system, and poorly funded wildlife organizations can do little to prevent damage from insensitive visitors. Divers and snorkellers should never touch or pick coral; most of the reefs remain undamaged, but the dead coral in the shallow waters on the shores at Wandoor is an early sign of what happens if coral is walked on or picked.

Shopping

Andamans is more a place to swim, breathe the fresh airs than shop. Nevertheless, Port Blair's markets have muti hued and multi sized corals and sea shell souvenirs for sale. Mother of pearl jewellery and artifacts, objects d'art in local wood and palm mats are also available.

Tourism Visions of Andaman and Nicobars

The limited scope for Industrial activity in the Islands coupled with the decline in the wood based industry pursuant to the Supreme Court judgment dated 7.5.2002 has led to tourism being identified as a thrust sector for economic development, revenue and employment generation in the islands. Keeping in view the fragile ecology and limited carrying capacity of the islands, the objective of A & N Administration is to strike for sustainable tourism.

The objectives

— To address the growing unemployment problem by placing thrust on promotion of tourism

— Total revenue generation being Rs.84 crores only (2001-2002) the future has to be planned with the objective of higher revenue generation.

— Promoting concepts of eco-tourism.

— To encourage private sector in tourism .

— To harmonise ecology & tourism for the benefit of the people of the islands.

Vision Statement

To develop Andaman and Nicobar Islands as an up market island destination for eco-tourists through environmentally sustainable development of infrastructure without disturbing the natural eco-system with the objective of generating revenue creating more employment opportunities and synergise socioeconomic development of the islands.

Vision targets

— Increase the earning from tourism sector

— Achieve the goal of high value low volume eco-tourist inflow.

Create employment opportunities for at least 1000 persons every year.

— Improve the status/quality of exiting hotels, tour operators and restaurants to the standards set by Govt. of India and UT Administration.

— Discourage un-approved tourism business etc.

— To create awareness and tourism consciousness among the islanders, specially stakeholders .

— Creation of adequate infrastureture in close co-ordination with concerned departments to ensure that tourism is sustained by an excellent foundation.

— Preserve the heritage and cultural traits of the islands and enable the development of rural societies.

— Sustainable development of different island destinations.

— Preserve the natural eco-system as a treasure.

Tourism Policy

The policies and guidelines of Government of India form the basis to promote tourism in Andaman and Nicobar Islands.

The Administration is focusing on the following issues:

— Promotion of high value low volume eco-friendly and environmentally sustainable tourism.

— Undertaking tourism activities, which are not harmful to the eco-system.

— To implement the master plan proposed by UNDP/WTO report for sustainable development of tourism in Andamans.

— Playing the role of a facilitator and encouraging private sector investment in development of tourism infrastructure.

— Gradual privatization of management of existing tourism infrastructure.

— Development of new tourism activities/products.

— Marketing A & N Islands as tourist destination at national and international level.

Strategic Framework For Promoting Ecotourism

The proposed Strategic Framework begins with a Vision statement aiming to sell Andaman & Nicobar Islands as the preferred tourist destination in South East Asia. From the vision statement, a three-pronged objective has been derived. These objectives aim to generate revenues and support the local population by developing a sustainable and competitive Ecotourism industry through promotion of the intrinsic values of the islands.

To create a sustainable, competitive Ecotourism industry in Andaman & Nicobar Islands, it is imperative to have a differentiated positioning for the islands. The positioning statement and the themes should act as the USP for the islands and assist in improving the awareness of enjoying the Mother Nature in a pristine way. Keeping this in view, the framework recommends that the focus theme be Health Tourism, with Tropical experiences, Adventure Tourism and Geo-cultural attractions following in that order.

Health Tourism can be defined as the gamut of services ranging from "The art of living" to the most authentic and original forms of yoga, meditation and Ayurveda, in the ambience of the ocean and the backdrop of lush forests. Health Tourism would be the strategic pull for the ever-growing, health conscious affluent from the west towards the sub-continent.

Apart from providing alternative ways of preventive, curative and rejuvenating processes through Health Tourism, imbuing the area's attractive flora and fauna, both in the sparkling oceans and the exotic tropical forests, and enjoying the unalloyed joy of adventure tourism can be strong pulls.

Recommended Course of Action

To attain the mission of branding Andaman & Nicobar Islands as the perfect destination for Ecotourism in South East Asia and positioning itself as an all-season health, nature and adventure tourism destination, a two stage strategic direction is recommended.

One, a set of short term initiatives to be carried out within the next two years that will bring Andaman & Nicobar Islands to a competitive platform in the tourism industry, and build capabilities to create a differentiated positioning as a Health Tourism destination.

Next, a set of long term action plans to be carried out in the next five years that would catapult the islands from the current state of an obscure destination to that of a preferred destination amongst the affluent markets of the west by concentrated marketing and branding initiatives.

As suggested, in the short term, the islands should build capabilities and capacities in all requisite areas. Capabilities of Health tourism can be imported from Kerala and customized for Andaman & Nicobar Islands. Capacity build-up in supporting infrastructure like transport, hotels, aqua-sports complexes etc (by benchmarking with the best in the industry) should be done in these two years.

Product development and packaging centered on the four themes needs to be strategically thought out. As short-term revenue generator, high value-low volume market development in mainland India is recommended. Involvement of public bodies in investments and in generating consciousness about Ecotourism is a pre-requisite.

Once the capabilities and capacities forming the backbone of the Ecotourism Industry have been built, market development in Europe and US by massive promotional and branding initiatives need to be undertaken. Aggressive marketing of Andaman & Nicobar Islands as The ultimate Ecotourism destination in South-East Asia, positioned around health is required. Use of Information Technology (eTourism) to promote the islands is also recommended.

The proposed strategic framework applied to tourism in Andaman & Nicobar Islands can be scaled up to develop tourism in the rest of India. Of course, the framework has to be modified to account for local Strengths, Weaknesses, Opportunities and Threats. Centric to this framework would be the identification of destinations that can be sold to the world as representatives of Indian tourism.

However, the forces promoting Indian Tourism are not potent enough. The industry needs a body like NASSCOM, which played a pivotal role in creating an image and selling the Indian software industry to potential customers. This body should be an association of the key stakeholders of the Tourism industry and not that of government representatives. It should include representatives from the tourism sector, hotels and restaurants, airlines, travel agents and representatives of local population.

3

Vulnerability of Island Environments

Since tourists spend money on travel, hotels, food, entertainment and recreation, they can be an important source of income and thus of economic development for islands with few other possible sources of revenue. The tourists who come to the islands have been attracted by their image of the island environment: sun and sea, white sandy beaches and waving palm trees, lush vegetation and friendly natives.

Tourism depends on the quality of the environment for its success, and good tourist development requires the protection and even the improvement of the environment. The most important tourism resources are the natural beauty of the island, their distinctive or exotic character, their recreation possibilities, and the cultural interest of the people. The hotels, resorts, transportation networks, recreation facilities and other tourism infrastructure can complement but never completely replace the dependence on environmental resources.

The basic problem with tourism development is that tourism facilities and the tourists themselves have impacts on the environment. If care is not taken, the tourism development itself can gradually destroy the environmental resources on which it depends. This problem can be particularly serious on tropical islands where the environment is fragile and easily degraded, and where the small scale of the island means that even moderate tourism development can have a proportionately large impact.

Environmental Impacts of Tourism

Tourism development usually starts with the construction of hotels, resorts and other places for tourists to stay. In addition there may be restaurants, night clubs, and recreation facilities such as golf courses, tennis courts, swimming pools, and marinas. These facilities require a lot of space, and land is usually scarce on an island.

Land and resources used for tourism are not available for other uses; developers may even want to keep local people away from beaches, reefs and lagoon areas reserved for tourists only. Whenever possible, tourism developers prefer to build on the coast, where the hotel will front on a beach and perhaps a coral reef, yet the coast is the most fragile and vulnerable area on an island, with the greatest conflicts between uses.

The construction of these facilities can have the same kinds of impacts as any other construction projects, such as soil erosion, changes in water runoff, and damage to natural environments. If the resort is on the coast, the plans frequently call for changes in the coastline, such as the creation or improvement of a beach, the construction of an artificial island, or the dredging of a harbour or building of a dock for tour boats to use to pick up and leave off the tourists. These changes may upset normal coastal processes and be very difficult to maintain. Coastal hotel sites themselves are often vulnerable to storm damage, erosion and other problems because of their exposed location.

Tourist developments also require resources that may be scarce on an island. Water may be in short supply, yet tourist use of water is usually much greater per person than among the local population. Tourists require large quantities of high quality food; if it cannot be produced locally, it will have to be imported.

The sewage from large hotels can be a source of pollution if it is not treated and disposed of carefully. Most hotel projects include waste water treatment plants, but these can be difficult to maintain in the islands and need to be monitored regularly. Tourist facilities also produce large amounts of solid waste which can add to the existing solid waste disposal problems on many islands.

Issue of Biodiversity Conservation

Tourism plays a crucial role in the economies of most Small Island Developing States (SIDS). Small island states such as Mauritius, Fiji, the Seychelles, the Dominican Republic and others have placed tourism as a top priority on their development agenda. Tourist revenues have grown especially important in light of plunging international commodity prices and falling fish catches traditional mainstays of island economies.

In the ephemeral world of international tourism the Republic of Seychelles has for many years remained the archetypal "island paradise", a seemingly perfect juxtaposition of sun, sea and sand. The country consists of one hundred and fifteen islands with a land area of 455 km^2, scattered as if by a giant hand over an Exclusive Economic Zone (EEZ) of over 1.3 million square kilometres in the

Indian Ocean. Of rugged formation and stunning scenic beauty, some seemingly rising straight out of the sea to great heights, the islands actually offer a tourism destination, free from tropical diseases, racial and religious disharmonies, and social upheavals.

Mahé is the most important island, about 27km long and up to 11 km wide. Other islands of major importance as regards to size and permanent population are Praslin and La Digue. The remaining seventy-four islands are all coralline. The economy of the Seychelles rests on tourism and fishing. Tourism accounts for some 20% of GDP and some 60% of total foreign exchange earnings In 1971, the number of visitors was 3175 as compared to some 128,000 in 1999. Today the official tourism strap line is " Seychelles, As Pure as it Gets"

Much of this 'purity' is perhaps because the Seychelles is a critical repository of some of the world's most interesting biodiversity, the original "Garden of Eden" (in the words of General Gordon of Khartoum fame). Over a thousand species of animal and plant life including the coco-de-mer and the giant tortoise are unique to the islands. Habitat range from mountain mist forests to coral reefs. These resources are the same assets that attract tourists: Their biological abundance is a key part of what makes the islands an alluring destination where visitors can experience relatively pristine natural beauty.

Whilst, some coastal environments have been damaged and a few marine sources have been overexploited by the tourism industry in Seychelles, the widespread ecological damage seen in other small island states has not been experienced as yet in the Seychelles. Habitat damage has made several other island states less appealing as destinations and has accelerated a boom-bust cycle in major tourist locations.

In the Seychelles environmental habitat protection was seen in the very early days of tourism as critical to the success tourism industry. The national parks of the Seychelles, particularly the Marine Parks were enacted primarily to protect pristine natural environments for visitors. One of the earliest protected areas to be promulgated under modern legislation was Cousin island. Cousin is also one of the earliest protected areas in Seychelles to be managed for tourism.

Biodiversity Conservation in Cousin Island

Cousin is a small, 27ha granite island. It lies approximately 4 km SSW of the North-eastern most point of the second largest granitic island, Praslin. The area is 27ha. It is physically dominated by a granite hill that rises to 69m, running directly into the sea on the rocky south and west coasts but is bordered to the north and east by a broad flat plain of phosphatic sandstone fringed by beaches of sand. The island has been privately owned for many years and was a coconut plantation from the 19th Century onwards. By the 1960's with the decline of the plantation-based economy in Seychelles, Cousin became a loss making venture.

In 1968, the island was purchased from the Seychellois owner by the International Council for Bird Preservation (an interntional federation of bird conservation organisations), now called BirdLife International, with funds raised through an international campaign. This was to ensure the conservation of endemic landbirds, particularly the very rare and threatened Seychelles warbler that was confined to Cousin and which numbered about 30 individuals in 1968. BirdLife International has managed it from its UK office until BirdLife Seychelles was created in January 1998.

In 1968 the island was designated as a Nature Reserve under the Wild Animals and Birds Protection Act. Furthermore, in 1975 it was designated a Special Reserve under the National Parks and Nature Conservancy Act, 1969.

The Special Reserve area includes the surrounding marine waters up to 400m offshore in all directions around the island. About 30 -100 hawksbill turtles nest annually on Cousin, the most important breeding site in the Western Indian Ocean for this species. Five terrestrial birds endemic to the Seychelles currently occur. Seven species of breeding seabirds nest in numbers exceeding one third of a million individuals. Neither rats nor cats, which have wiped out many indigenous faunas, have been introduced to or colonised the island.

The main conservation achievements on Cousin are listed below.

— Restoration of the entire native lowland forest as well as other indigenous vegetation.

— Rescue of the Seychelles warbler population from extinction, and translocation to two other islands.

— One of only four islands where a viable population of c 1000 Seychelles fody is maintained

— One of only three islands where a breeding population of c.20 of the critically endangered Seychelles magpie-robin has been established.

— Restoration of the hawksbill turtle breeding population to make the site a globally important one.

— Restoration of breeding seabird populations to make it one of the most important seabird rookeries in the W. Indian Ocean.

— Restoration of endemic and indigenous invertebrates and reptile populations.

— Maintenance of the highest coral reef fish biomass in the granitic islands

— Maintenance of the site as one of only four islands in Seychelles free from alien vertebrate predators such as rats and cats.

— Reduction in poaching of endangered species to almost zero, and maintenance of good community relations.

— Reserve management and decision-making by locals.

Educational activities through tourism bring eight thousand to ten thousand visitors a year. The island is open to visitors four times a week but there is no overnight accommodation. Entry to residents is free; foreign tourists pay a landing fee. Reserve management since 1984 has been entirely by local staff based in situ. In 1998, BirdLife Seychelles was set-up and registered as a non-profit local association under Seychelles law and led by nationals. BirdLife Seychelles took over all ongoing projects of BirdLife Interntional including the management of Cousin island. The management policy has remained awareness-oriented and non-interventionist, the principal aim being to protect globally threatened biodiversity.

Mangaing the conservation program: In 1998, with the creation of the local NGO, BirdLife Seychelles, Cousin was integrated into the conservation program of this organisation. In 1999 a new Management Plan was introduced. The Vision for the Reserve is laid out in the new plan as follows. "It is the intention of BirdLife Seychelles to make Cousin Island Special Reserve the best marine and terrestrial small-island protected area in the world". Several goals are laid out in the plan:

1. Maintain the integrity of the island ecosystem as a place rich in biodiversity, especially rare and threatened species sensitive to Man-induced impacts, in a financially sustainable way.
2. Improve the richness of the biodiversity through management based on sound science.
3. Use Cousin as a showcase for ecosystem and species conservation and extract maximum benefit for education and public awareness.
4. Improve the understanding of the island ecosystem and its components through long-term monitoring programmes.
5. Build human and physical resources to undertake all the above roles on Cousin and elsewhere in Seychelles.

It has been recognised that the vision and goals as quoted above can only be achieved if sustainable financing mechanisms are being put in place. Nevertheless, it is to be noted that the primary objective of Cousin Island is not and will never be a means of generating income. It is a unique island ecosystem that offers a richness of biodiversity that needs protection under all circumstances and at all cost. This biodiversity can however be used as showcase and maximum benefits for education, public awareness and coupled with that, income generation can be provided in a sustainable manner.

Cousin is a very popular tourism destination. It receives almost 10% of all visors arriving in Seychelles. Because of Cousin's potentially high tourism interest, BirdLife does not market the island and wants to maintain it as a 'well kept secret'. It is BirdLife Seychelles' policy not to encourage any increase in tourism activities on the island. The marketing of Cousin island and the handling of tourism operations from the main islands to Cousin are undertaken by private tour operators. A colour brochure was produced in 1999 but acts primarily as an information guide to visitors prior to landing on the island. BirdLife Seychelles restricts itself to maintaining and selling all tickets to the island, and its wardening staff control tourism landings and tours on the island itself.

The island is open for public visits on 4 days a week, namely Tuesday – Friday. Mondays are used for general island maintenance, staff training, educational visits, special visits by overseas missions, etc. During its 4 opening days the island was occasionally closed due to bad weather conditions or public holidays. Closures amounted to one day per month on average in the FY1998/1998 representing an additional average of 600 potential visitors.

Tickets for Cousin Island are sold by BirdLife Seychelles in several ways, through Bwa Mare, a local ornithological and nature guide based on Praslin Island, a small percentage on Cousin Island itself (primarily from private yachts), or through a credit voucher system which BirdLife Seychelles has established with major tour agents such as Masons Travel, TSS and Mahe Shipping (for cruise ships and private yachts). In 1999, over 60% of all tickets were sold through the Praslin ticket agent.

In the period examined, a substantial number of clients arrived on Cousin Island through Masons Travel, a large Seychellois-owned tour operator. For its Cousin operations, Masons Travel sub-contracts other smaller local operators based on Praslin. Visits to Cousin Island are mostly organized as part of a full day excursion to different satellite island around Praslin. lt accounts for an average of 55% of the Cousin clientele. Small and medium sized Praslin based boat operators that may work in collaboration with other local tour operators, such as Kreol Holidays or TSS account for some 38% of clients. The balance is provided through chartered yachts or cruise ship visits. All tourists are guided by Cousin Wardens. There are no preferential systems in place for boat operators. Any boat operator licensed by the Seychelles Licensing Authority and the Ministry of Tourism can ferry visitors to Cousin.

Typically, a tourist boat will arrive off Cousin carrying anything from 5 to 30 visitors depending on the size of the vessel. They are then ferried to the beach in a small reserve boat operated by the Wardens. This prevents the accidental introduction of alien species that could harm the native biodiversity. Visitors are taken to a small shelter featuring some interpretative material and are broken into smaller groups according to their favoured language: English and French are spoken by the Wardens.

The tour takes visors to special features of the island. The character of the island changes according to the two main seasons of the year. Species such as Noddy terns and Hawksbill turtles nest only at certain times of the year. The tours typically last for one an a half hours. After the tour is over, visitors gather in the shelter and are ferried back to their boats.

BirdLife Seychelles undertook a visitor survey on Cousin during 2000. The survey was designed to provide information on the origin of visitors, the quality of the visit and the biodiversity seen, and willingness to provide increased financial support through increased fees or sales and donations.

About 500 visitors responded to the questionnaires. On the aggregate level the results indicate that the quality of the experience was high. The majority of visitors found the tour interesting, informative and well organised. Most if not all the visitors though that the island was being very well conserved. As well, they agreed that adequate information was received about the island. Thirteen percent of the respondents however felt that the time on the island was insufficient. With the financial questions, only 38 percent felt they would be willing to pay more for a visit to Cousin. Twenty-nine percent of all the respondents indicted they would buy souvenirs if these were available and were of good quality. The survey confirmed the anecdotal evidence and the many superlatives in the island's Guest Book that visitors are well pleased with the Cousin experience and that moreover feel that conservation objectives were being met.

Tourism on Cousin is controlled through certain management practices. These include the following.

— No boats are allowed to land on the island or moor on the reef. Only the Reserve small (6 metre) fibre-glass boats can offload passengers.

— All boats have to moor offshore on a sandy-bottom area

— The island is open to limited visitations only; 4 days a week from 9.30 am to 4 p.m. and is closed on all public holidays and weekends.

— Visits are designed to be short. Visitors stay a maximum of 2 hours on the island. Full day trips or overnight accommodation are not available. Impacts such as use of freshwater and sewerage management are thus minimised.

— Trails for visitors cover only part of the island; they avoid sites of certain breeding species which may be sensitive to human disturbance, such as Bridled Terns.

— All visitors have to tour the island with a Reserve Warden. Self-guided walks are not possible.

— Flash photography is not allowed.

— Smoking is not permitted

— Barbecues, picnics and similar activities are not permitted.

— Trails are examined on a regular basis for erosion or other physical impacts.

— Visitors are kept at a distance of at least 3 metres from nesting sea turtles.

— Populations of flagship species such as the Seychelles magpie robin, the Seychelles warbler, seabirds and sea turtles are routinely monitored by scientists and wardens.

— Visitations are terrestrial-based. Visitors normally do not have the time to snorkel on the reef. Scuba diving is uncommon within the Reserve boundaries.

— Being a Special Reserve under Seychelles laws various other restrictions apply such as complete ban on fishing and on collection of any materials

Owing to the restrictions described above, few impacts are observed. This is well demonstrated by a study comparing the breeding success of Fairy terns nesting along the paths to those further inland. The results showed no difference between the two. Similarly, populationss of hawksbill turtles, fish and seabirds have increased or at the very least stabilised. However some impacts are possible. These include the following.

— Certain species may become too habituated to humans.

— The visitor experience may be decreased on certain days when too many groups land on the island.

— Wardens have a decreased ability to carry out other tasks owing to their tourism functions.

— Some anchor damage has been observed.

A survey to gauge community attitudes to Cousin and to tourism there is being designed and will be implemented by 2001. Meetings and discussions undertaken in 1999 by BirdLife Seychelles with boat operators and community groups and business leaders on Praslin, do indicate a sophisticated knowledge of Cousin activities and of other protected areas nearby. In general, these groups strongly supported Cousin tourism operations as conservation values were apparently well understood and benefits flowing to local business and communities were perceived. People did not feel at all excluded from the tourism industry at a national or local level, although many wanted the Government to introduce a more streamlined country-wide system for licensing, tax benefits and other incentives.

To date, Cousin Island generates all its revenue from controlled tourism activities. The management authority retains all the revenues for the purpose of managing the island for conservtion. The only monies available to BirdLife Seychelles to run Cousin island Special Reserve are those generated from tourism.

Benefits to communities and stakeholders: Economic benefits of Cousin to surrounding communities and private sector are impressive. Educational tourism to Cousin is serviced by Seychellois-owned travel agencies, and several other local small to medium sized operators and charter boat businesses based on Praslin. The employees of these businesses, apart from cruise ships, are in the majority all

Seychellois. It is estimated that some SR.3 million (US$ 600,000) is generated from these activities through direct and indirect revenues.

Unlike tourism in many other developing countries, much of the proceeds flow to local businesses. In addition, all the staff employed on Cousin are from Praslin. A few live on Cousin with their spouses in free housing provided by the island management. It is the policy of BirdLife Seychelles to source all provisions, materials and services for the island from Praslin. All in all, Cousin forms an important part of income generation in the surrounding communities.

Open access to resources leading to the 'tragedy of the commons' underlies the continued exploitation of the environmental resources in the Seychelles. Many communities and persons still view the islands with a frontier mentality, i.e.: environmental resources are boundless and can be used by anyone for any purpose. Because of this, compliance to environmental laws in Seychelles has been historically poor. In addition, enforcement has been weak, complicated by a small island mentality and society 'where everybody knows or is related to everyone else.'

However, poaching of resources by communities surrounding Cousin is very low compared to other protected areas nearby. The main reason may be that tourism has benefited the nearby communities as described above. In addition, poachers may not feel comfortable about entering an area containing tourism activity. A third reason for low community pressure is the local management of the island. The wardens are all residents of the nearby island of Praslin, and have managed to negotiate a "poacher-free" zone around the island with their compatriots on Praslin.

This is in contrast to the neighbouring Aride Special Reserve which has very limited tourism and is managed by expatriates; poaching remains at an all time high, so much so that the Reserve management has requested funding for high-tech surveillance and anti-poaching equipment. Effective protection of the fringing reef around Cousin by its wardens has been scientifically proven to have maintained a reef fish community of high diversity and biomass.

The best incentive to manage Cousin is of course its outstanding biodiversity, a result of Birdlife management. There are few conservation examples in Seychelles where quantified indicators can demonstrate a substantial change in environmental quality wholly due to management intervention. There are several instances on Cousin; the transformation of the coconut plantation into what is believed to be an ancestral coastal forest, the 300% increase in population of the Seychelles warbler, the increase in numbers of nesting hawksbill turtles, and finally the significantly higher fish biomass on Cousin reefs compared to other MPAs in the area.

As an island containing an abundant and diverse biota, the benefits of Cousin to research are obvious. Groundbreaking research undertaken on Cousin has led to publications in the most prestigious scientific journals in the world including Nature and Science. Other benefits include Cousin's reputation as one of the region's great conservation success stories. Tourism is partially responsible for these successes through revenue generation and other benefits.

The economic benefits of tourism on Cousin to the management authority are growing. The island is financially self-sufficient and this therefore frees BirdLife funds for other conservation work. Revenues not utilised in direct management of the island are presently being used to pay for a local staff namely a Program Assistant, a Technical Officer and an Education Co-ordinator for BirdLife Seychelles. Remaining funds are being set aside in a small trust fund. Thus Cousin Island is supporting the wider conservation program of BirdLife Seychelles.

Future Plans: The plans for tourism on Cousin are intimately twinned with national tourism trends, activities and policies. For example, a ceiling on the number of tourists entering the Seychelles was established in the early 1980's, thus curtailing the predictable flow of mass tourism to sensitive sites such as Cousin.

Ownership of substantial sections of the tourism industry by the Seychelles Government and by local operators, both large and small, and an emphasis on upper-end of the tourism market has also ensured that local people value tourism as well as the importance of environmental protection to this industry. The co-habitation of tourism and environmental protection in these islands has to a certain extent buffered the inevitable impacts that infrastructual development accompanying tourism have on natural habitats.

Nevertheless, with an expanding local entrepreneurship base and more operators entering this industry, meeting the needs of Seychellois and tourists, and weighing economic and environmental realities is, like what happens in natural ecosystems, a delicate and difficult balancing act. For example the specific objectives are the Seychelles Tourism Policy 1995 – 2000 are:

1. to foster general economic activity through foreign currency earnings

2. improve balance of payment and increase foreign exchange earnings
3. create a positive international image for the country
4. enhance communication between people and reduce insularity of the nation

The current Government policy is to main:ain an up-market image of the tourism product. It also recognises that the tourist market is a rapidly evolving one and there could be further scope for further growth of new categories of tourists, especially with regard to recreational and scientific visitors. Along with investments in haut gamme establishments, the Government has stated that it would encourage small investors to enter the sector to create a broad base of private operators. Concomitant with this policy, Government is determined to shift from what it calls the present passive marketing strategy stressing sun, sea and sand to one which will integrate a wider range of more dynamic activities and attraction. In this type of situation the Cousin experience can be valuable.

Because of Cousin and other similar protected areas with successful tourism ventures, it is now well recognised that tourism can be a positive force for biodiversity conservation. However, it is also believed that such sensitive sites, need controlled visitations and management of numbers. At a national level this is accepted and thus there is no pressure on BirdLife Seychelles or other "managers of eco-tourism" to increase visor numbers. A national Tourism Master Plan has been produced with a strong emphasis on the symbiosis between environmental management and tourism. Government is in fact urging owners and managers of small islands to maintain a small but very high quality product.

Nature tourism in the Galápagos Islands

Planned and organized nature tourism began in the Galápagos Islands in 1967 when Lindblad Travel, a New York-based tour operator, brought in the first tourist vessel, a 66-passenger Chilean ship. Considerable advice for the design of the tourism programme was provided by the Charles Darwin Foundation for the Galápagos Isles (CDF) over the several years prior to and after that time.

The Foundation felt strongly that nature tourism represented the economic activity that was by far the most compatible with conservation of the archipelago's biological diversity, evolutionary and ecological processes, and environment. Since then tourism has grown gradually in the islands, particularly during the 1980s and 1990s, reaching the present total of over 60,000 visitors per year and almost 90 tourist vessels. Nature tourism has become by far the greatest economic force in Galápagos. The vast majority of other activities are dependent upon or closely related to it.

There are a number of natural limitations which have major implications for tourism development in Galápagos:

— Potable water is severely limited

— Soils are marginal or poor and there are few mineral resources

— Supplies of construction materials are severely limited

— Disposal of solid and liquid wastes is very difficult

— The climate is cool seven months of the year.

— Beaches are not attractive for recreational tourism

— The islands, because of location, are expensive to visit compared to many areas

— The real attraction for visitors is the fascinating and awe-inspiring experience of seeing the unique and abundant wildlife, which is truly wild yet fearless of humans

— At the same time, the islands' ecosystems and species are generally extremely fragile and vulnerable to the activities of humans, and especially to the impacts of human-introduced species

The first four of these, to some extent modifiable through technology, place significant limitations on the development of tourism support centres and services, if the environment and biodiversity are to be conserved, especially in the regions around those centres, but also well beyond them because of the problems of introduced species. The remaining five taken as a whole are why Galápagos tourism will never be competitive with models of recreational tourism practiced in other major regions of the world. To preserve its unique attraction and niche, Galápagos tourism must be designed and practiced in an extremely careful and controlled manner to both guarantee protection of ecosystems and ecological and evolutionary processes, and maintain and maximize the unique educational and high quality nature tourism experience that the islands offer.

Legal and institutional framework

Nature tourism operates in the Galápagos within a fairly well-developed legal and institutional framework, which has been evolving over the past 40 years. The Galápagos National Park, established by law in 1959 and including approximately 97% of the 7,800 km2 total land area of the archipelago, has been under the active and generally improving management of a specialized governmental arm of the national forestry, protected areas, and wildlife institution since 1968. Management is guided by a Management Plan, the first one prepared in 1975, with major evaluations and revisions in 1984 and 1996.

The Galápagos Marine Resources Reserve was originally established in 1986, covering all the inner sea and 15 nautical miles outside a baseline connecting the outermost islands. A Management Plan was finished in 1992, but due to lack of jurisdictional clarity in various laws, inter-institutional conflicts in the tripartite commission established to manage it, and pressure from certain economic sectors, no real active management began until late 1996, when the National Park began to take certain initial actions to protect it.

International recognition and support for conservation of the Galápagos Islands has been substantial. In 1978 it was approved as the world's first Natural World Heritage Site under that international convention. In 1984 the terrestrial part of Galápagos was nominated and accepted as a Biosphere Reserve, under UNESCO's Man and the Biosphere Programme. The CDF was also established in 1959, as an international non-profit organization with the following key responsibilities:

— Establishing and managing the Charles Darwin Research Station (CDRS, 1960 onwards)

— Conducting applied research aimed at conservation problems

— Facilitating scientific research on a broader scale

— Act as chief advisor to the government of Ecuador on Galápagos conservation

— Environmental education on Galápagos at local and national levels

— Training of Ecuadorian scientists and conservation managers

— Garnering and channelling international support

The Galápagos National Park (GNP) administration began to function in 1968. It is in charge of management of the National Park (terrestrial), with full legal support of the government, and has developed considerable administrative autonomy. The GNP also has begun to try more actively to protect, patrol, and manage the Marine Reserve, under the new Special Galápagos Law enacted in early 1998. The Reserve has been enlarged to 40 nautical miles outward from the baseline connecting the outermost islands, making it over 130,000 km^2 in size.

It is now the second largest marine reserve in the world, after the Great Barrier Reef National Park of Australia. The Reserve is to be overseen by a Marine Reserve Commission, under the new law, but the Park has been placed specifically in charge of its protection and management, to which the other institutions are supposed to contribute support and expertise.

The legal and institutional basis for management of tourism in Galápagos is basically functional, but still somewhat confused. The 1998 law made some improvements, but did not remove that confusion. The parent institution of the National Park (INEFAN - Ecuadorian Institute for Forestry and Natural Areas) at central government level issues permits or *patentes* to operate in the National Park (terrestrial) to tourism operators. However, another institution, the Merchant Marine (DIGMER), issues separate permits to operate vessels in Galápagos.

Although not very active in Galápagos, the National Tourism Corporation (CETUR) supposedly controls the quality of visitor services on the vessels in relation to prices charged. Over the past three decades this situation has meant that the Park Service itself does not directly control the granting of permits for tourism vessels to operate in Galápagos. Instead it has tried to manage the itineraries and other aspects of management or use of Park visitor sites by those vessels once the operator begins activities in the archipelago.

Moreover, even INEFAN has frequently found itself in the position of having to grant permits due to *fait accompli* arguments, since operators have been able to get the DIGMER permit for navigation first, then argue that they have permission and have made the economic investment, so must have a permit to operate in the National Park.

In the Marine Reserve the situation is not entirely clear in relation to visitor snorkelling and diving sites. The Park has designated a large number of sites, but there are no detailed regulations legally established for their use, in contrast to the terrestrial visitor sites. In effect, the National Park is beginning to manage those sites, but its legal basis for and management and control of them is still weak.

Nature protection strategy

The key tenets of the strategy for protection of nature in Galápagos, both in general and in relation to nature tourism in particular, are as follows. These have been formally enunciated by the Ecuadorian government both through legislation and in various general and specific plans for conservation of the Galápagos:

- Maximum protection of biodiversity and ecosystems, both terrestrial and marine, because of their total interdependence
- Preservation of evolutionary and ecological processes
- Ensure a high quality educational experience for visitors
- Recreational and educational opportunities for the local population

In designing nature tourism management in the Galápagos National Park used and still adheres to several specific principles:

- For every visitor site selected for visitation, ensure that there remain 3-4 similar sites not to be visited.
- Concentrate impacts in fragile areas to protect the physical environment and vegetation (i.e. by the use of marked trails)
- Zero tolerance for impacts on reproductive success of wildlife (also by marked trails with certain distances from breeding colonies maintained)
- Impacts should be monitored, especially biophysical ones

Evolution of nature tourism in Galápagos

During the first few years of tourism development in the islands, approximately 20 terrestrial National Park visitor sites were established and the basic design for their use and management was established. Over the following 25 years the system has been refined and augmented with additional terrestrial sites and a set of marine ones, and additional regulations established based upon monitoring results.

However, the core design is still the same. The following subsections describe the salient characteristics of that system at present.

Zoning of the national park and visitor sites

- *Extensive Use Zone*: 11 visitor sites on 7 islands, for groups of up to 16 visitors, one group at a time (these sites are used by smaller vessels)
- *Intensive Use Zone*: 21 visitor sites on 15 islands; for use by a larger number of groups at a time (these are used by large, medium-sized, and smaller vessels)
- *Recreational Zone:* 19 sites on 4 inhabited islands; for use by local residents and visitors seeking less expensive alternatives for recreation, education, hiking, and camping
- A total of 53 terrestrial visitor sites, representing less than 1% of the National Park area

Zoning of the marine reserve for tourism and visitor sites

- 64 Marine visitor sites have been designated
- Most are Extensive Use (groups of up to 16 persons, one group at a time)
- A few are Intensive Use
- Most are for diving, a few for diving and snorkelling, and a few others for small launch rides
- The National Park's jurisdictional and legal control is still weak
- The National Park is in early stages of defining management for these sites and activities

Trail system

Most Extensive and Intensive Use Sites have marked trails, approximately 1-1.5 m. wide, in order to protect fragile vegetation, geological features, and erosion-susceptible substrates; to protect potentially sensitive wildlife while at the same time affording excellent, close-up nature observation; and to concentrate biophysical impacts to soils and vegetation to very limited, manageable areas (the trail beds). Smaller numbers of less fragile visitor sites in the Extensive and Intensive Use Zones, such as some beaches and previously disturbed (by human settlement) areas have designated open areas (with marked boundaries), instead of trails. Visitor sites in the Recreational Zone are mostly of the open type. In the Marine Reserve the visitor sites have no underwater trails, and a few have or soon will have buoys for securing diving and snorkelling launches (prevention of anchor damage).

Guides system

Naturalist Guides are required for all visits to the Intensive and Extensive Use visitor sites. They are not required for visits to the Recreational Zone, except for organized tour groups of non-locals. Naturalist Guides are licensed by the National Park, after taking required training courses given by the Park and CDRS and passing an examination. The guides' main functions are to be interpreters and to apply the Park's regulations for visitor control; they also serve as the Park's "eyes and ears" in many situations, reporting as required on infractions, making natural history observations, and conducting monitoring. Park regulations require a maximum of 16 visitors per guide in a single group.

There are three categories of Naturalist Guides, defined by formal educational preparation, experience, and the type of training course and examination passed. The highest category is for those with university degrees in the natural sciences (biology, geology, or similar) or natural resources management, and the lowest requires no formal education whatsoever beyond basic primary education. The resulting quality of guiding ability in terms of natural history and, conservation biology interpretation is highly variable.

Tour modalities

Most visitors use vessels as floating hotels, which are called Navigational Tours, and include Diving Tours. Smaller numbers stay in local hotels and go on Day Tours, mainly to the central islands' visitor sites, because most Day Tours operate out of Puerto Ayora, Santa Cruz Island, which by far the major tourism support base in Galápagos; small numbers do the same out of Puerto Baquerizo Moreno, San Cristobal Island. Even fewer visitors go on local Bay Tours in the areas surrounding the local ports, especially at Puerto Ayora, and some at Puerto Baquerizo Moreno. Very small numbers of tourists are starting to visit Puerto Villamil on Southern Isabela Island for either Day Tours or Bay Tours. Port Tours - in which cargo vessels bring tourists to Galápagos from the continent, take them through Galápagos from one inhabited port to another and then back to the continent - are now rather rare, but still occur occasionally.

Key regulations

— All types of tour operations require authorization by the National Park.

— All Navigational, Diving, and Day Tours have fixed itineraries established by the National Park (the intent is to avoid congestion at the most popular and heavily visited sites, mainly in the more central islands, and to disperse vessels to underused sites.

— Terrestrial sites may only be visited during daylight hours (camping areas in the Recreational Zone are an exception) and a detailed set of conservation regulations apply.

— There is not yet a detailed set of regulations developed and applied for marine visitor sites.

Annual operational fees paid by operators to the national park

The Navigational Tour operators pay annual permit fees at three levels, according to the number of passengers they are authorized to carry, the quality of services offered, and the type of itinerary:

— Level A: $250/year x number passenger spaces

— Level B: $200/year x number passenger spaces

— Level C: $150/year x number passenger spaces

Day Tour operators pay at two levels, according to the same three criteria: $150 or $50 x the number of passenger spaces.

Apart from this permit and fee collection system, there is no real system of concessions yet developed for Galápagos by the responsible Ecuadorian agencies.

Key indicators of success of the system

There are several key indicators which demonstrate the basic soundness and success of this nature tourism management strategy. First, the level of protection of biodiversity, ecosystems, and the physical environment is extremely high. Studies prove only minor impacts on soils and geological features at very restricted locations and on certain trails, all of which have been easily manageable through special structures such as wooden stairs at two sites, or maintenance of trails at a few others.

Long-term studies of impacts on key indicator species such as waved albatrosses, three species of boobies (blue-footed, red-footed and masked), and two species of frigatebirds (magnificent and great) at both visitor sites and non-visited control breeding colonies have shown no detectable impacts on reproductive success over several decades. Likewise, studies of visitor motivations and actual and desired experiences in Galapagos have shown that the quality of the visitor experience has been maintained at an extremely high level so far .

Major tourist trends and indicators

There has been a gradual increase in numbers of visitors to Galápagos over three decades, with major increases in numbers in the late 1980s and mid-1990s, which coincide with major increments in the number of vessels in operation.

A typical trend seen in nature tourism around the world - ever increasing development forced by operators. Unless the management authority truly controls both the entire planning and concessions process, with systems in place for defining desired future conditions, selection of indicators and standards for those, and monitoring of the indicators to determine the limits of acceptable change, there will always be gradual and continual increase in infrastructure, modalities, and new types of activities and equipment being added to the system. Likewise, concessions systems must be controlled by the management authority, or it will be trying continually to keep up with and accept changes brought from the outside. This inevitably eventually leads to congestion, conflicts among user groups, and a decrease in the quality of the originally defined visitor experience.

By-products of Nature Tourism

The great economic boom in tourism has produced four major related trends in Galápagos. These indirect by-products of nature tourism are severely threatening the islands' biodiversity and ecosystems:

— Rapidly growing human population

— Rapidly increasing rates of introduction of alien species

— Rapidly increasing demand for local resources

— Massive extraction of some resources (marine fisheries)

These trends and efforts to counteract them are discussed in much greater detail elsewhere in this volume. They are presented here only to indicate that the situation forms part of the context within which nature tourism operates in Galápagos, and continued unplanned growth in tourism would continue to exacerbate the trends and undermine conservation efforts.

The following are a summarized list of the main future threats to the generally successful and well-managed nature tourism system in the Galápagos. These have been identified over the past 4-5 years by myself and other specialists in nature tourism management in protected areas, as well as at a workshop on the re-zoning of the GNP and redesign needs of the tourism system at the CDRS/ GNP in 1993, attended by representatives from the tourism industry, the National Park, CETUR, the Navy, the CDRS, and many other organizations. For the purposes of this chapter they are presented as a list with some added comments, where appropriate. They are not in any order of priority. Most of them already exist as initial problems, but which have not yet become major threats.

— *Inadequate zoning of National Park, Marine Reserve, and rural and urban areas.* The last Management Plan revision improved it, but it still needs to take into account a broader spectrum of recreational/educational opportunities, based upon protection needs for biodiversity and natural resources and desired visitor experiences, founded upon the proper combinations of biophysical, social, and administrative (management) settings to be created and offered.

— *Imbalance in visitor site use*: congestion at some visitor sites & under-use of others. The National Park has been improving this gradually through management of fixed itineraries, but there is still more to be done.

— *Unplanned appearance of new tourism modalities*: e.g. Day Tours, Bay Tours, Sport Fishing Tours. This will continue to occur until the National Park directly controls the entire planning process and concessions system.

— *Unplanned appearance of new tourism activities,* such as jet skis, sport harpooning, and helicopter overflights. Again, these may be unavoidable unless the National Park really controls the entire planning process and concessions system.

— Increasing number of newer operators less sensitive to conservation needs.

— *Decreasing quality of guiding.* There are now approximately 200 licensed guides and the quality is very variable, from extremely good to very poor. Some visitors are starting to voice complaints and the poorer quality is beginning to affect the visitor experience. The entire system of classifying guides, and training and licensing them, has become somewhat politicised by some of the guides, local interest groups, and politicians. The classification system, qualifications for guide candidates, training curricula, requirements for obtaining a license, and a process for evaluation of guides need to be redesigned.

An inadequate concessions system:

— Weak government control in general and lack of direct control of the system at Galápagos National Park level.

— Industry usually well ahead of management authorities, with new modalities and activities being introduced without planning or control by the Park.

— Inadequate development of the needed partnership between government (the National Park) and the nature tourism industry.

— Tourism supply capacity is almost double the actual demand, yet the tendency is for more growth.

— An open-ended economic growth system in the nature tourism industry, which the Park authorities do not really control. Studies and experience worldwide amply demonstrate that this will lead eventually to increasing social conflicts between visitor groups, a notable decrease in the quality of the visitor experience, ever more infrastructure and undesirable development, and, in the special case of Galápagos, the basic resulting problems of rapid population growth and increasing rates *of* arrival *of* introduced species. The answer is not to create monopolies, but a well-designed oligopoly *of* tourism operators, balanced among local smaller ones and larger ones from the continent, totally controlled by the National Park and managed according to a well-designed concessions system with clear and fair regulations and processes. The tourism industry should be brought into the process of planning and design of that system, or primitive *laissez-faire* capitalism will lead to implosion of the nature tourism system in Galapagos.

— Lack of cohesiveness in the tourism industry. Suspicion and primitive competition dominate, exacerbating the situation described in the previous point.

— Lack of adequate conflict resolution and consensus building among all stakeholders in the process of planning and designing tourism management in Galápagos.

— Lack of adequate presence of the GNP at visitor sites.

— Lack of adequate interaction of a GNP specialized tourism staff with visitors.

— The range of experiences offered to visitors is too limited.

— Growing conflicts between the tourism industry and local populations.

— Increasing strain on GNP management capacity if the nature tourism industry continues to expand.

— Economic displacement of local tourism operators by economically more powerful outside ones from continental Ecuador.

— Inadequate planning, monitoring, and evaluation processes, based on measurable indicators and standards, for the entire nature tourism system.

— Gradual breakdown in the quality of the unique visitor experience offered by Galápagos.

Lessons from the Galápagos ecotourism

The following are the main lessons provided by the Galápagos tourism experience, as well as related experience in other countries, such as Costa Rica, Mexico, the United States, Canada, Australia, and New Zealand, after nearly 30 years:

1. An adequate concessions system is a major key to long-term success, with these main characteristics:
   - Maximize control at local management authority level.
   - Design of the entire system, not just parts in piece meal fashion, is critical.
   - The system requires a solid legal basis: a decree or law, regulations, clear and open procedures, an operations manual, and knowledge by all stakeholders of the process.
   - The local management authority must have the true capacity to apply consequences for infractions, ranging from warnings, to fines, and even to loss of permits to operate.
2. Management capacity must be in place before tourism growth is allowed.
3. The system must be planned and then closed to further development once limits are set.
4. All stakeholders must be part of the process of planning and implementation, including the tourism industry.

5. Opening of the system to additional growth must be based upon monitoring of key indicators and standards, established as part of the design and planning process, and the decision should be taken only by the management authority, based upon such technical grounds.

Future strategies

The new Special Law for Galápagós, approved in early 1998, contains numerous provisions to enable starting to try to dampen those trends. The law is still somewhat weak in various places, but at least it puts the key subjects on the table and provides for a beginning. Details will have to be worked out by elaboration of the regulations to be derived from the law, with all stakeholders participating and agreeing to abide by those rules or suffer the consequences. The key components are:

1. Immigration control: partial, but the principle is established.
2. Quarantine and control system to sharply curtail introductions of alien species.
3. Greatly increased support for the National Park and to strengthen local authorities, the educational system, etc.
4. For the Marine Reserve
   - Increased to 40 miles around baseline connecting outermost islands
   - Single authority for administration and management (GNP)
   - Industrial fishing allowed only in two zones outside previous 15-mile limit and for one more year; then should stop.

— New management plan.

— Fisheries restricted to locals (artisanal) and with strict new regulations to be developed.

Future strategy for nature tourism management

The main components of this strategy flow from the problems and threats and lessons learned, presented previously:

1. Redesign and restructuring of the concessions system
2. GNP must have direct control of concessions system
3. Refinement of zoning to include the Marine Reserve and rural and urban areas
4. Planning process including all stakeholders
5. Redesign of guide classification system, and guide training and licensing
6. Include greater range of visitor experiences in zoning and visitor site redesign
7. Institute improved planning, monitoring, and evaluation process based on measurable indicators and standards
8. Management capacity must exist before any increases in tourism are permitted, and only be allowed when technical monitoring of pre-established indicators and standards demonstrate the acceptability of such (within the limits of acceptable change established in the planning process, in light of the defined desired future conditions)
9. GNP must decide when to open, modify, or close parts of the system

Provisions of the new law affecting nature tourism

The new Special Galápagos Law does not directly confront most of the main problems and future threats to nature tourism in Galápagos. It does, however, contain a few provisions worth noting:

1. It places full power for authorizing tourist operations in Galápagos protected areas in INEFAN, via the GNP (a positive step, but needs refinement so that direct control will reside in GNP).
2. No transfers of permits will be acceptable except to local residents.
3. No new permits for tourism operations can be issued, unless revised GNP Management Plans determine such.
4. Provision for favourable treatment for local tourism operators.
5. Certain limits on new tourism infrastructure in non GNP areas (e.g. hotels). INGALA (Galápagos National Institute Council) will have control of this aspect, creating potential for conflict with the GNP.
6. Some confusion is present in the law among roles and power of INGALA versus INEFAN (GNP).

Planning Environment-Friendly Tourism

One major question to be answered in planning tourism development is what scale of tourism is appropriate for the local environment and culture. Every place has a carrying capacity that cannot be exceeded without bringing about serious changes or even the collapse of important resources or systems. While some small-scale tourism can be fit in almost anywhere, large scale tourism can cause major problems if it is not planned very carefully.

The number of tourists an area can absorb should be decided before tourism development goes to far, because there always will be pressures for bigger and bigger developments. The appropriate scale of tourism may be determined by the most limited resource, such as water or coastal land, or by the desire to prevent serious social or cultural impacts. How many people, for instance, can a community receive comfortably as visitors, or how would it feel to be outnumbered by the tourists on your own island?

Unlike most development projects that only involve a specific site or area, tourism frequently depends to some extent on an entire country or island. It is therefore in the interest of the tourist industry to see that the overall planning of the country's development includes the requirements of tourism.

As more governments begin environmental planning and make physical plans (including town plans, master plans and coastal zone plans), it is essential that these plans include the sites of particular scenic or recreational potential. The coastlines, vistas, swimming beaches, waterfalls, mountains and lagoons that tourists visit and photograph are capital assets just like hotels, but they are generally not owned by the tourism interests that benefit from them. Only careful comprehensive planning, and often the understanding and support of the traditional owners, can protect these resources from degradation and destruction.

Planning helps in making choices between conflicting uses, or in finding ways to make them compatible. It should aim to locate unsightly or polluting activities, like industrial areas, fuel storage depots, rubbish dumps, etc., where they will not destroy the beauty of a town or coastline or conflict with tourist sites. In many island towns, there are already too many cases where urban pollution is making tourist beaches unsightly or unsafe. Planning early for tourism development can help to avoid damaging and expensive errors and also to prevent the gradual erosion of environmental values significant to tourism.

Improvements that help tourism, like better transportation, tree planting, restoration of historic sites, urban beautification and cleanliness, also improve the environment for the local population. Tourism development can help to stimulate general community improvement.

Conservation

One area where tourism interest coincides with the long-term interest of a country is in the conservation of nature and traditional culture. Tourists are particularly attracted by unusual vegetation, birds and wildlife, by coral reefs and lagoons, and by distinctive cultures, customs and life styles. Very little has been done to develop these resources for better tourism, and ways need to be found to make them available without putting them at risk or degrading them.

The development of protected areas such as national parks and reserves can be one way to protect a country's heritage and to make it available for local education and tourism. The investment in facilities such as trails, signs, picnic shelters and visitors' centres is usually repaid through tourists who come in larger numbers and stay longer because there are more things to see and do. Conservation areas will also attract special categories of tourists with interests in botany, bird watching, wildlife, nature photography, skin diving, archaeology, etc. Such kinds of tourists are generally more interested in the country they visit and less apt to cause serious social impacts.

Infrastructure Requirements

Any major tourist development requires a good airport where large jets can bring tourists from overseas countries. Visits by tour ships may require improved docking facilities. Roads may have to be built to resort sites, or improved for tour buses. Water and electricity supplies may have to be increased. All these kinds of infrastructure require investments which must be added on to the direct cost of a tourism project.

Building roads, airports and docks can have major environmental impacts which are beyond the scope of this unit. Their overall effects, however, may be positive as well as negative. Such facilities benefit local people as well as tourists, reducing the isolation of remote areas and increasing the convenience of travel within the country and overseas. Tourism development can thus support useful expenditures that could not be justified for the local people alone.

Damage from tourist use

Tourists are often unaware of how fragile some island environments are. They may trample vegetation and thus cause erosion, or disturb birds and wildlife. They may leave their rubbish behind, littering the environment. They are apt to break corals as the walk or swim over the reef. Even anchoring in a fragile reef area can result in significant damage to corals. Tourists love to collect corals, shells and other pretty objects as souvenirs, but too much collecting can damage a reef or other site. Fishing is sport for a tourist, but it may take away resources needed as food in nearby villages.

Where a few tourists may do little damage, thousands of them can be a disaster. Think of the difference between one tourist breaking off a piece of coral, and hundreds of tourists each taking a piece of coral; a reef could quickly be stripped of its corals and shells. Areas subject to heavy tourist pressure should be protected from damaging activities. Laws may be needed to protect wildlife and to control collecting.

The increasing demand for curios such as stuffed turtles, turtle shell jewelry, mounted butterflies, and traditional objects made with rare bird feathers or animal skins can threaten rare species with extinction. The manufacture and sale of such objects should be prohibited or strictly controlled. Coral, shells for handicrafts or collectors, and local trees used for carving can also be wiped out locally or reduced to low levels when too much is used to supply the tourist trade.

4

Socio-cultural Dimensions

Since 1950 tourism has grown about five percent per year into the largest global industry representing ten percent of world GDP and employment and seven percent of capital spending. This same period has witnessed the reorientation of small tropical island economies away from traditional export staples like sugar and copra toward mass tourism development, related construction and financial services. Nowhere has this transformation proceeded further than in the Mediterranean, Caribbean and Northern Pacific destinations, the so-called "Pleasure Periphery" of Europe, North America and Japan.

Recent research, however, has emphasized the socio-environmental damage of over-rapid mass tourism development particularly in the smaller more accessible and popular resort islands. In the Mediterranean, such negative impacts have included deforestation, beach alteration, near-shore pollution and reef destruction, and paralyzing summer crowding and other socio-cultural intrusions that threaten insular lifestyles and identity. In the Caribbean, the scarring of mountains with condominium developments and road networks has caused widespread erosion and wildlife extinction.

The concentration of large infrastructure and resort complexes along delicate coastlines has destroyed mangroves and beaches and caused lagoon pollution from sand mining, dredging, and sewage dumping. In popular Pacific destinations, delicate mangroves have been harvested for construction material and reefs severely damaged by visitor trampling and collecting.

About three-fourths of small countries are islands of less than one million inhabitants. Small islands suffer from a constellation of limitations. These include lack of diversification because of resource scarcity, income volatility because of extreme openness and export concentration, and an inability to generate self-sustained growth because of capital shortage and small market size. Remote islanders also suffer reduced real income and basic services because of high transport costs associated with dependence on essential imports and scale diseconomies exacerbated in archipelagic states like Bahamas, Maldives and Kiribati. As a result, island economies are among the world's most vulnerable, i.e. susceptible to potential adverse external shocks beyond their control.

Unique natural and cultural patrimony constitute the one enduring insular comparative advantage. It is not thus surprising that island microstates have made mass tourism development their primary postwar modernization of choice. This strategy seems particularly germane during the present era of globalization when the colonial economy based on preferences is crumbling, and when post-cold war political realignments have resulted in significantly reduced center-periphery aid flows. However, insular environments are notoriously fragile, characterized by high endemism but weak species diversity (resistance), making them pervious to external impacts from introduced predators, overharvesting, invasive crowding and natural disasters.

Similarly, closely interlocking insular terrestrial and marine ecosystems are extremely vulnerable to the kinds of large-scale resort and transport infrastructure construction necessary for mass tourism to thrive. Likewise, with the decline of renewable agroforestry and fishing pursuits, traditional cultural roots have been weakened by the presence of affluent visitors and lifestyles and the lure of Western media.

As a result, after a generation of mass tourism development, island bio-cultural diversity around the world is under siege posing a major threat to the long-run viability of tropical tourism. For example, the majority of global bird extinctions have occurred on islands. Although over one of six plant species grow on islands, one of three of all known endangered plant species grow on oceanic islands. This is partly the outcome of development thrusts and partly a legacy of neglect. Oceanic islands are underrepresented worldwide in protected areas.

The outlook is similar in the peripheral island areas. After extensive colonial clearing of virgin forests for sugarculture and later bananas, the Caribbean, the region most dependent on tourism, bears the scars of overrun. Freshwater resources are threatened by hotel and condominium developments on steep slopes, harming watersheds, causing erosion and lagoon pollution. Nearly 30 percent of the reefs–a good barometer of environmental health–are at high risk because of runoff and sedimentation and discharges of untreated municipal and hotel waste.

The large number of pleasure yachts and cruise ships directly inject waste into these waters because of inadequate port reception facilities. The highest threats appear to be in the smaller Lesser Antilles, precisely those destinations most aggressively promoting and dependent upon mass tourism.

Partly as a result of these intrusions, 60 species of endemic birds are endangered plus 30 mammals and 37 reptiles. Since 1985, fish catches are off nearly 50 percent in gross tonnage.

The situation is similar in the Indian Ocean. Heavily populated areas have been plagued by overfishing, reef harvesting for trade in rare species, sand mining for construction, as well as mangrove destruction, erosion, siltation and coastal pollution through unplanned urbanization. Deforestation in Comoros is proceeding at over five percent per annum. The natural vegetation of Mauritius has been virtually eradicated for sugarculture. Mauritius and Seychelles are ranked second and third in the world in terms of endangered native plant species.

In some islands over half of the endemic species are threatened. In Mauritius 62 animal species (mainly birds) are extinct. In Seychelles rapid declines in rare turtle populations continue. In addition, beach-based resort and infrastructure facilities are under threat from sea level rise in Seychelles, Mauritius and Maldives.

The Pacific, in transition from subsistence to a cash economy, is undergoing over-grazing, intense cropping on marginal hillsides, unsustainable logging and land clearing for commercial agriculture. Deforestation rates are among the most rapid in the world. The region also boasts the largest number of documented bird extinctions in the world and seven times more endangered species than the Caribbean.

The coral reef system, most extensive and diverse in the world, is under pressure from all sides: overfishing, dynamiting, sand extraction, fertilizer and sewage pollution, and the destruction of fringing reefs and mangroves for coastal tourist and urban development. With increasing globalization, world affluence, transport access and the demand for authenticity, pressures on island biodiversity and traditional cultural mores are expected to escalate.

Why has the short-run 'success' of mass tourism been allowed to jeopardize island bio-cultural diversity and the industry's long-term future? The answer lies in the peculiar nexus between a tourist-environment scale disequilibrium and a free-market political economy.

First, the imposition of a large-scale, untrammeled consumption-based international throughput economy atop a tiny, delicate, finite island ecology almost guarantees over time that insular carrying capacities will be crossed. This scale discrepancy is due to the high-volume profit imperatives of heavily capitalized airline, cruise, and hotel interests plus other secondary effects associated with rapid mass tourism development in small destinations: loss of traditional sustainable resource activities, mounting waste and crowding from on-site visitors, and environmentally altering construction of large-scale resorts and infrastructure.

Second, island policy makers with short electoral time horizons are often preoccupied with increasing visitor volume instead of maximizing net local expenditure. To protect market share in the competitive global marketplace, they favor rapid growth, extending the shoulder season, and even price discounting with tour operators. Such policies place further pressure on the already stressed socio-environmental fabric and lead to increasing promotion, crowding and decay followed by declines in profit margins, visitor and vacation quality, and the resources needed to refurbish and restore.

A third element in the mix is the complex and dynamic nature of tourism itself. Its impacts are asymetrical. To illustrate, visible economic benefits are quick to appear and linear while socio-environmental costs are non-linear and usually surface after dangerous thresholds are reached. This benefit-cost disjunction is partly why the "Sustainability Diamond" is rarely achieved. Normally, early in the resort cycle the needs of the visitors and the developers/travel interests take precedence, and the priorities of the host population and bio-cultural asset protection are deferred until "tourism as usual" becomes unsustainable.

A final problem is that tourism's impacts are difficult to measure. They are pervasive, involving a series of products/services consumed through time, and they include difficult to quantify cultural and ecological externalities. There are no universally accepted comprehensive measures of overall tourism impact. As a result, island decision makers cannot easily assess where their destinations lie along the tourist-environment continuum, and thus they cannot proactively anticipate danger points.

Economic and Social Impacts

The economic and social impacts of tourism are a big subject that cannot be covered thoroughly here. They should be examined in detail for any large tourism development project. Economically, tourism can create jobs for local people and bring money into the country. However many tourists like their comforts from home, and it is often necessary to import a large part of their requirements, so that much of the money may leave the country again to pay for these imports. If the resorts and hotels have been financed by overseas investors, they will also want to export their profits.

The developers may want the government to improve the airport, roads and other infrastructure, and possibly to provide tax breaks and other financial advantages, which cost the country money. The remaining benefit to an island country from some kinds of tourism development may thus be small indeed. Other kinds of tourist facilities provided by villages or financed locally may be economically more interesting.

The social impacts of tourism may also be important. Most jobs for local people in the tourist industry are as servants, house maids, waiters, gardeners and other menial work that may give people a sense of inferiority. At the same time the tourists come from other societies with different values and lifestyles, and because they have come seeking pleasure, they may spend large amounts of money and behave in ways that even they would not accept at home. Local people seeing the tourist example may want to live and behave the same way. Tourists may also, out of ignorance or carelessness, fail to respect local customs and moral values. These and other social effects may be among the most important long-term impacts of tourism development.

Tourism in Economic Development of Small Islands

Small island developing states must orientate their national development policies outwards to the rest of the world. This is an imperative, not an option. Their narrow range of resources, the constraints imposed by their small populations and land areas, and their limited technical capacity demand it. The lure of tourism to them stems from its natural comparative advantage over other potential sectors of the economy.

As per capita incomes steadily rise, tourism has become the largest industry in the global economy. According to the World Travel & Tourism Council (WTTC), it accounts for 11.5 per cent of the world's GDP and 12.5 per cent of its employment. Small island states have long benefited from this growth: in some Caribbean nations, for example, tourism employs as much as 25 per cent of the workforce, contributes some 30 per cent of GDP, and provides the bulk of foreign exchange earnings.

Tourism is expected to go on growing by some 5 per cent a year. World Tourism Organization (WTO) projections suggest that international arrivals will soar from 594 million in 1996 to 700 million in the year 2000, and 1 billion in 2010. The vast majority of tourists will continue to come from the developed world, but it is not too far-fetched to imagine that economic expansion and per capita income growth in populous developing countries - such as Brazil, China and India - will, over the long term, provide considerable impetus to the upward trend. This outlook makes tourism one of the most competitive sectors of the global economy.

In order to enhance the long-term viability of this critical sector, many small island developing states have embarked on forward-looking strategies to improve efficiency and strengthen coordination through such regional mechanisms as the Caribbean Tourism Organization and the Tourism Council of the South Pacific. Specific measures in the proposed Sustainable Tourism and Development Plan for the Caribbean include:

— Fostering common definitions and measurement criteria for sustainable tourism so as to effect quality control within the industry.

— Expanding facilities for training and sharing information.

— Upgrading marketing strategies and deepening tourism research.
— Creating the necessary enabling environment for tourism development through market- based incentives and appropriate regulatory frameworks.
— Linking tourism directly to the islands' cultural and ecological assets.

Linking Tourism and Development

The movement towards a more holistic approach to the link between tourism and development owes much to the work of the WTO. It also received a major boost from the United Nations Conference on Environment and Development (UNCED) held in Rio in 1992, and the Global Conference on Small Island Developing States (SIDS) in Barbados in 1994, which examined the development of tourism within the broader context of sustainability. The implementation of agreements from such global conferences often falls short of expectations, but they have a great impact on raising consciousness of issues of international concern as they foster a vital consensus for national and global action.

Coordinating Concerns

The preparatory process for the SIDS Conference produced a vast inventory of research and information-sharing on all aspects of the development problematique of small island states. It fostered critical review and coordination of the issues among concerned groups, including civil society. And it raised the level of commitment to national objectives and ownership of them. This would otherwise have been difficult to achieve.

The Conference's main outcome, the Barbados Programme of Action - which was endorsed by the United Nations General Assembly - outlines the strategies and policy actions required at national, regional and international levels to meet the challenge of sustainable development of small island states. It recognized tourism among 14 areas identified for priority action, alongside such other key resources as land, energy and biodiversity.

Their limited development options - and heavy dependence on this fragile sector - make SIDS particularly vulnerable. They are at risk both from economic dislocations in the tourists' home countries, and from such environmental shocks as hurricanes or other natural hazards, which can quickly wipe out the progress built up over many years. Economic diversification may provide a desirable buffer to such eventualities - but it is likely to be a medium-term option for only a few.

Conscious of the industry's competitive climate, SIDS have increasingly focused on upgrading the quality of their tourism product - and on emphasizing its uniqueness through niche marketing of ecotourism and nature and cultural tourism. They have also given special attention to improving the management and protection of tourism assets, disposing of wastes and combating land degradation.

The Barbados Programme of Action will be reviewed at a Special Session of the General Assembly in September 1999. This will provide a timely opportunity to assess how well it is being implemented and, particularly, identify what can be done to improve things in those priority areas where only limited progress has been made. The Commission on Sustainable Development (CSD) will act as the Preparatory Committee for this review at its seventh session in April 1999, when it will consider tourism and oceans, both specially important to small island developing states.

Coasts and Oceans

Oceans are the life-line of tourism. So SIDS are very concerned with the sustainable management, use and protection of coastal and ocean resources. They follow with particular concern such activities as the regional and global conventions and protocols relating to the Law of the Sea, the International Coral Reef Initiative, the Climate Change Convention, the Global Programme of Action for the Protection of the Marine Environment from Land-based Activities, and the trans-shipment of nuclear wastes through the fragile marine ecosystems of such international waters as the Caribbean Sea.

The CSD will share national experiences, especially in implementing strategies to integrate environmental and social considerations into the concept of sustainable tourism. This new focus, defined by the Organization of Eastern Caribbean States, offers guiding principles that apply to all SIDS: 'Sustainable tourism development is the optimal use of natural and cultural resources for national development on an equitable and self-sustaining basis to provide a unique visitor experience, and an improved quality of life through partnerships among governments, the private, and local communities.'

Sharing information

This approach aims at forging links with a wide variety of stakeholders in such areas as the environment, health, agriculture and culture, the private sector, trade unions and local communities - consistent with the pervasive impact of tourism in SIDS. Sharing information and coordinating institutions will be critical in managing this outreach, but timely support is now available through the Small Island Developing States Network (SIDSnet): this Internet-based facility, developed by the United Nations Development Programme in close collaboration with the Alliance of Small Island States, promotes the exchange of information on the environment and sustainable development among 42 island developing states in the Pacific, Caribbean, Indian and African regions.

This embracing concept of tourism holds much promise. But implementing it effectively will largely depend on whether tourist bodies in SIDS have the organizational capacity to make these partnerships work. Building this capacity may well be one of the most fruitful areas for international assistance.

Travel and Tourism in the Global Marketplace

Travel and tourism has been acclaimed as the world's largest industry and generator of jobs. The work it provides through hotels, restaurants, car rentals, taxi operators and tour guides is obvious enough. But the many less obvious jobs which it creates - through the linkages to agriculture, renewal of urban and rural communities, cultural revitalization and heritage preservation - are even more critically important to developing economies.

Tourism can be like a rising tide for developing countries. It has the potential to float every boat. It can be the driving force of activity in every sector of the economy: agriculture, industry, construction, transport and infrastructure development, as well as education, sports, culture and entertainment. A growing tourism industry serves to drive local demand and expand the local market in every single sector.

This high propensity to create wealth in diverse economic sectors - and to distribute it among all strata of the population - has been one of tourism's most compelling attractions. It has led governments and economists of the South to adopt it as a focal sector for diversifying their economies, which have historically depended on producing primary raw materials, often just a single crop. It generates high-paying jobs across the spectrum. And intensive central investment in tourism facilities has the indirect effect of creating opportunities for the sustainable development of hundreds of small- and medium-sized ancillary businesses, which are not capital-intensive, in a variety of fields. But it would be a terrible mistake for us in the South to regard tourism as an alternative to competitive agriculture or to the value-added production of other goods and services. We must see it as a growing sector in a competitive global marketplace. It needs to meet the challenges of globalization. The tourism market is not dominated by comparative advantage, exclusively driven by economies of scale, patented technology and low wages. Instead, natural and cultural features, knowledge, the social environment and product differentiation all give rise to their own niche markets.

Role of tourism in the development of Caribbean Islands

The Caribbean has been one of the world's most successful regions in using tourism for transforming its economies, improving its social and physical infrastructure and increasing its people's quality of life.

Research conducted by the World Travel & Tourism Council (WTTC) shows that travel and tourism in the Caribbean - which is supported by some $15.4 billion of capital investment - is expected to have generated $32.5 billion of economic activity in 1998. It will have contributed 24.7 per cent of the region's GDP and accounted for 25.1 per cent of its direct and indirect employment. In addition, and very important to the Caribbean Governments, travel and tourism is expected to have produced $7.8 billion in revenue - 25.9 per cent of the total taxes they collect - while only receiving in return $2.0 billion - 19.8 per cent of government operating expenditures.

The WTTC also says that Caribbean travel and tourism is expected to grow at 6.3 per cent per annum - or 108.2 per cent in real terms - between 1998 and 2010. Is this sustainable? Rather, what must be done to sustain this level of economic activity without consuming the natural and cultural environment - the very core product on which it depends? These questions were addressed at the 1992 Earth Summit in Rio, which produced Agenda 21.

In 1996, the WTTC, the World Tourism Organization and the Earth Council joined to launch an action plan entitled Agenda 21 for the Travel and Tourism Industry: Towards Sustainable Development. Regional seminars were held in London and Jakarta in 1997 to increase awareness of the programme and to adapt it for local implementation. And a Think Tank Seminar on Agenda 21 for Travel and Tourism was held in the Caribbean from 3-5 December, 1998 on the small, 945 square-kilometre island of Dominica, between the French islands of Martinique and Guadeloupe.

Formerly a British colony, and now an independent state of the CARICOM region, Dominica is the last Caribbean island to have preserved a vast amount of its rainforests. In all, 21 per cent of its area is legally protected as wildlands within its National Park and Forest Reserve System. In December 1997 UNESCO deemed Dominica's Trois Pitons National Park - once described as 'a priceless living laboratory where scientists can study tropical biology in a primitive state' - to be of universal importance to mankind, and therefore listed it as a World Heritage Site. Dominica is also the home of the last remaining indigenous Carib people of the islands of the Caribbean.

Economic transformation

In 1996, the Government of Dominica and Green Globe entered into an agreement to develop Dominica as the Caribbean's first Green Globe Destination. It has a population of just under 80,000 people of which 3,500 are Caribs, and attracts some 68,000 stay-over visitors. With its 700 hotel rooms, mostly in cottage type hotels of under 50 rooms, its World Heritage Site, some world-class diving sites and a growing reputation as the Nature Island of the Caribbean, Dominica is emerging from its wilderness onto the tourism highway. It hopes, through tourism, to transform its banana economy to a more sustainable level.

The statement of the Prime Minister, the Hon. Edison James, quoted on page 15, could apply to all small island developing states and succinctly encapsulates the realities of the South. The Government's strategy, as laid out in its official policy, 'is aimed at maximizing the benefits of tourism without compromising our social values, while ensuring the preservation of our environment and ecosystems.'

If they are to achieve these objectives, developing countries must focus on using their indigenous music, exotic foods, culture, art and crafts, and on adding value to them. And they must similarly preserve and restore indigenous architecture, natural heritage and the environment.

Tourism must become a matter of national pride for each citizen. Each developing country, no matter how small or how vast, must aim at becoming a world-class tourist destination for its quality, service and value for money. And each country must have a dynamic positive and comprehensive Tourism and Hospitality Education Agenda in place to underpin these goals.

Long-term investment

The task ahead is enormous, the challenge to developing countries as they seek to achieve world competitiveness in tourism is staggering. The South cannot do it alone. Private sector investment will go a long way in establishing those tourism facilities and infrastructures which demonstrate that they will produce an early payback.

But gigantic sums will also have to be invested in long-term sustainable projects for restoring and preserving the environment, and in upgrading facilities for health and education and the services needed for the world-class competitive tourism standards that will have to be achieved. Ensuring the sustainability of local economies and peoples must be at the core of any strategy.

North-South economic cooperation must now place tourism on a top-priority agenda. The sentiments so eloquently and passionately articulated at the Rio Earth Summit of 1992 must be backed up by a flow of financial resources to implement sustainable travel and tourism activities in the economies of the South. The valves of the Global Environment Facility must be opened up to allow the resources to flow smoothly.

The lessons from our painful experiences in agriculture, mining and industrialization must not be dissipated. Now is the moment - and tourism is the opportunity. The North must seize this moment to do things right this time around.

Reefs and reforms

Just over a quarter of the coastlines of the countries of Latin America and the Caribbean are potentially highly threatened with degradation from coastal development; just under a further quarter face a moderate threat. The growth of tourism is cited as one cause of increasing stress; others include domestic sewage, coastal erosion, industrial waste, mining and the run-off of sediment.

Tourism has long been recognized as an important part of the social and economic development of the Wider Caribbean. It depends heavily on the health of the region's marine and coastal ecosystems and of the living resources that inhabit them. Caribbean coastal areas enjoy unique levels of biodiversity: a high proportion of species are native ones. The Caribbean hosts the largest barrier reef in the Western Hemisphere, stretching some 220 kilometres long, off Belize, and is home to almost 60 per cent of the world's scuba diving tours.

Need for integration

The Caribbean tourist industry has grown rapidly over the last decade. In 1996, it received 25.5 million visitors - of which 10.7 million were passengers on cruises. This growth has shown that tourism must be more integrated into planning and management.

Sustainable tourism development requires the adoption of sound environmental practices. Coordinated approaches are needed to resolve conflicts over resources, involving all stakeholders. Information must be shared, instruction materials made available and incentives provided.

The direct and detrimental impacts of tourism are usually known, but have not been quantified. So better information is needed about the carrying capacity of ecosystems, the impacts of tourism on them - and the benefits gained from environmentally sound practices.

Promoting sound management

Governments in the region established the Caribbean Environment Programme (CEP) in 1981 as an integral part of UNEP's Regional Seas Programme, to conserve and promote sound management of the marine environment. Through a regional coordinating unit in Kingston, Jamaica, UNEP functions as Secretariat for the Cartagena Convention and its Protocols, as the Caribbean's only regional environmental treaty.

The CEP has embarked on a project to support and improve environmental practices in the tourism industry in the region. The Caribbean Environmental Network project is aimed at achieving the optimal use and maintenance of coastal and marine resources as part of a sustainable tourism strategy. A joint venture with the United States Agency for International Development in Jamaica, it is designed to improve the quality of the environment and protect resources in the Wider Caribbean by promoting the use of environmentally sound practices by the tourism industry and reducing its impacts. To this end, the CEP has developed close partnerships with key organizations, involved in many aspects of tourism, from the private, public and academic sectors in the region.

Among its activities to support the development of tourism as an environmentally sustainable industry are:

— Promoting best management practices and applying clean technologies within the tourism industry, particularly the hotel sector.

— Implementing training programmes, with associated manuals, to strengthen the capacity of people in the tourism industry to manage solid wastes and wastewater, contribute to integrated coastal area management and to site and design tourist facilities appropriately.

— Implementing pilot demonstration studies on minimizing the impact of tourism development in the coastal and marine environment.

— Producing publications like booklets, manuals and technical reports on key topics of interest for disseminating in the tourism industry, and thus building awareness.

Other regional organizations have also begun programmes to improve the environmental practices of the tourism industry. The CEP contributes to these efforts to promote tourism as an industry that is not just environmentally, but also economically and socially, sustainable.

Role Tourism in the Development of Mediterranean

The framework of UNEP's Regional Seas Programme lends itself particularly well to examining the relationship between tourism and sustainable development. Many of these seas are popular tourist destinations, receiving a massive influx of visitors. This is particularly true - and has long been so - for the Mediterranean, where tourism is a major challenge, with a significant economic, social and environmental impact.

The Blue Plan, one of the elements of the Mediterranean Action Plan, has highlighted the main trends of tourism in the Mediterranean Basin. This work has served as a basis for the activities of the Tourism Group of the Mediterranean

Commission on Sustainable Development (MCSD) whose conclusions were presented and adopted at meetings in Antalya (Turkey), and Monaco in September and October 1998.

In 1990, 135 million tourists stayed in the Mediterranean coastal regions, including 75 million from abroad - mostly from European countries - representing around 16 per cent of all international tourism. Nearly all the countries in the region benefit from the growth in international tourism, if to varying degrees. It accounts, for example, for more than 8 per cent of Spain's GDP, 7.5 per cent in Tunisia, 7 per cent in Greece, 22 per cent in Cyprus and up to 24 per cent in Malta.

The MCSD has also found that the proportion of international tourists compared with the permanent population of the coast has risen continually in the region since 1980 - reaching 299 per cent in Malta. Foreign currency earnings from tourism contribute substantially to the balance of payments, going a long way to compensate for trade deficits. In Tunisia, for example, it covers some 70 to 80 per cent of the deficit, though the precise figure varies from year to year. In Turkey, foreign currency earnings from tourism represented 25 per cent of all exports in 1997.

But there are huge discrepancies between countries in the amount of revenue gained and jobs created, and inequality in the development of tourism. France, Italy and Spain together account for 80 per cent of revenue from the region's international tourism. But countries like Tunisia and Turkey have witnessed a very rapid growth in the last 20 years. Revenue from tourism accounted for 25 per cent of Turkey's exports in 1997, and 60 per cent of the Balearic Islands' GDP.

This growth creates large numbers of jobs and halts emigration, but also changes traditional societies, introducing them to often very different ways of life and consumption models, and transforming the social use of space.

The impact of tourism on the environment and landscape is very dramatic at first glance. Shorelines are destroyed by new infrastructures, marinas and urban expansion, and by the increase in population (with its need for wastewater and waste disposal) and the pressure on water resources. Outstanding habitats, like dunes, are degraded. A very fast pace of development can aggravate this. The Mediterranean islands provide a physical illustration of the problem of overloading: this appears to be a core issue of sustainable development, although this has been disputed.

Demands for quality

But tourism can have positive environmental effects. Tourist demands for a quality environment, especially for clean bathing water, are a powerful lever for improving water purification facilities and solid waste disposal in popular areas. There is a growing trend towards diversification as tourists discover the region and nature through ecotourism.

In 1998, the MCSD carried out 21 in-depth case studies of a representative sample of destinations, with the support of the countries, the local authorities and the relevant economic and environmental non-governmental organizations. These showed that the following should be considered when drawing up action plans to incorporate tourism into sustainable development:

Different treatment should be given to:

— Old tourist development areas, which come within rehabilitation initiatives.

— Areas under development, which often require a review of existing programmes to improve control, especially of their impact on the environment.

— Quasi-greenfield areas, such as Libya and Albania, which often represent major environmental challenges: their future tourism development should be carried out with particular attention to sustainability.

— Special attention should be paid to the legislative framework for land use within the context of integrated coastal area management: many countries have passed laws banning construction within 100 or 200 metres of the shore. Without appropriate planning that takes environmental considerations into account, the conflicts surrounding tourism developments will only increase.

— Financing environmental protection through money from tourism has led to some promising experiments. Some countries, such as France and Tunisia, have introduced public land acquisition initiatives.

— Institutional and professional capacity-building to make tourism and the environment more compatible presents another major challenge, especially at local level.

A series of recommendations on tourism and sustainable development should be adopted at the fifth session of the MCSD in Rome in June 1999. The MCSD's preliminary work will also provide substantial input to UNEP's contribution to the work of the seventh session of the United Nations Commission on Sustainable Development.

Ecotourism as a Tool for Sustainable Development

Ecotourism s increasingly recognized as a tool for sustainable development. Achieving genuine ecotourism is a challenge, as high standards have to be met. But when it is achieved, communities and natural environments are the immediate beneficiaries.

Though the word 'ecotourism' has only come into common use in the last 10 years, it describes a goal towards which entrepreneurs, government agencies, non-governmental organizations (NGOs) and communities have been working for more than two decades. A short definition put forward by The Ecotourism Society in 1991 describes it as 'responsible travel to natural areas that conserves the environment and sustains the well-being of local people.' Professionals working within the field of ecotourism generally agree that it is characterized by:

— Travel to a natural area.

— Travel that supports the conservation of biodiversity.

— Travel that brings benefits to local host communities.

— Travel that leads to greater understanding of the natural or cultural environment visited.

Including these four components in a travel package significantly restricts the number of products that can genuinely be labelled ecotourism. Many confuse the term with nature tourism or adventure travel, but they are not the same. Rather, ecotourism is one niche market within the larger, and rapidly expanding, nature tourism market. By our estimates, nature-based tourism now comprises 20 per cent of the world travel market, and ecotourism 7 per cent.

Ecotourism is not just visits to the rainforest. It can be activities in a traveller's home country, as long as these visits are responsible and benefit conservation efforts and local communities - and the visitor has participated in some learning experience. One example might be camping at a national park, paying an entry fee, following park rules of conduct, buying supplies at a gateway community outside the park, and participating in a natural history lesson.

A crucial role

There is an encouraging 'greening' of mainstream tourism, and this trend should be supported at every opportunity. Greater sustainability in the industry as a whole will have the largest impact on overall environmental protection, and on communities and individuals. But ecotourism will play a crucial role in the communities and natural environments under the greatest pressure from development. These include rural, often indigenous communities, and 'pristine' natural environments such as coral reefs, tundra and rainforests - the destinations that ecotourists want to visit.

Daily the demand grows for these unique cultural and natural resources to be brought into the global economy. As this pressure increases, ecotourism can help make the process more beneficial, empowering communities and their resource managers with an alternative to more invasive practices.

Ecotourism, of course, is no panacea. Indeed, it introduces its own set of problems. Such impacts as cultural erosion and atmospheric pollution are ever-present, as in any tourism product. Planning and managing destinations, setting up institutional partnerships and the continued development of environmentally friendly technology will provide some solutions.

Ecotourism institutions and professionals easily form alliances with their cousins in sustainable tourism, and in the larger sustainable development community, and there should be greater interaction between them. The Ecotourism Society is among the institutions working on this by bringing ecotourism professionals together and facilitating communication with other sustainable development partners such as conservation NGOs, government tourism and resource management agencies, community groups and the private sector. The Internet has been invaluable to this process, facilitating a much easier exchange of ideas, and enabling the society and other organizations to teach professionals and institutions about the field.

Balancing Commercial and Ecological Interests

This section examines tourism on the island of Tasmania with particular focus on the apparent balance achieved between commercial and ecological interests. As such, Tasmania represents an example where there may be lessons for successful sustainable development in the tourism sector, contrary to the many examples throughout the world where tourism development has had negative impacts on the economic, social, cultural and ecological components of islands.

Tasmanian tourism development may provide a basis for comparative analysis of what appears to work well and what does not. It is not suggested that Tasmania is the only example of apparent sustainable development in tourism. Bermuda represents what must surely be considered a success story in tourism development when compared with most Caribbean islands.

Butler describes the relatively successful case of the Shetland Islands in controlling the development of its tourism. The Shetland case points out some interesting parallels with Tasmania: relatively small numbers of tourists compared with their 'mainland' counterparts; strong local control over tourism development; product attributes centering primarily on the natural environment, history, and culture of the island, all in addition to the normal island characteristics of access constraints, vulnerability due to extensive coastlines and limitations due to costs and infrastructure.

However, too often, the literature on island tourism reflects the dismal failure of tourism development to delivery economic benefits while at the same time preserving cultural and natural environments. Butler warns that this situation can result in a superficial acknowledgement of environmentally appropriate development whereby tourism development occurs in areas where it probably shouldn't or at the very least without any real control or managed under the banner of environmentally sound development.

> What is being criticized is the hypocrisy and cant which is pontificated about tourism saving the environment through non-impacting forms of ecotourism, which is all too often an excuse for introducing tourism into areas where it may have been more appropriate for it not to have ventured, or where it should only have been allowed under conditions of control and management. Controls are exerted on most forms of activity yet tourism is one which frequently seems to avoid them, beyond those imposed on the actual construction of projects and appropriate labor and safety laws. Using the green banner and misusing the concept of sustainable development does not seem to make for what has also become termed 'appropriate' tourism.

He argues that tourism development, if it is to be truly environmentally appropriate must demonstrate the following characteristics.

> ...tourism which is developed and maintained in an area (community, environment) in such a manner and at such a scale that it remains viable over an indefinite period and does not degrade or alter the environment (human and physical) in which it exists to such a degree that it prohibits the successful development and well-being of other activities and processes.

Thus, the more appropriate form of tourism is that which exists within the context of sustainable development and not, as is so often the case, the prioritization of tourism itself which is sustainable.

Tasmania, or Van Diemen's Land as it was known until 1856 when it became a self governing colony of England, consists of five main islands: Tasmania; Bruny; King; Flinders; and Macquarie. The main island of Tasmania lies 240 kilometres south of the Australian mainland, separated by the infamous Bass Strait. In total, Tasmania represents less than 1% of the Australian landmass at 67,800 square kilometres and has a population just under 500,000. A higher proportion of Tasmania is set aside for parks and reserves than any other state or territory in Australia. Tasmania has more coastline per unit area than any other state or territory in Australia, approximately 5,400 kilometres.

It is a mountainous island, the highest peak being Mount Ossa at 1,617 metres. The interior of the island is dominated by the Central Plateau which contains thousands of small lakes as well as the Great Lake and Lake St Clair, Australia's deepest lake. Tasmania's climate is temperate with annual precipitation exceeding 2,500 millimeters in the west of the island and declines as one goes further to the east coast. The summer mean temperature is 18C and winter is 8C with a significant amount of variation from north to south and by altitude.

The generation of hydro-electricity, logging and timber production, mining, agriculture including winemaking, and some fishing are the principal economic activities on the island along with tourism. Transportation links are well developed and include a comprehensive road network throughout the island except in the Wilderness Heritage Area in the southwest. A state owned ferry service provides regular service from Melbourne to Devonport on the north shore as does a private high-speed catamaran service between Melbourne and Georgetown at the mouth of the Tamar Estuary leading to Launceston. Launceston's location in the north east of the island makes it the most important terminus for freight shipments both by sea (50%) and air (80%). More than half of all air passengers to Tasmania fly into Hobart.

Historically, Tasmania occupies a unique place within European history. Its first non-indigenous settlement was as a penal colony. Van Diemen's Land, along with Devil's Island in French Guianea, was the epitomy of human misery and cruelty in the 19th century. This reputation as one of the worst places to be incarcerated ensures that the island enjoys high awareness among Western and particularly, British Commonwealth peoples. This awareness, ironically, forms the basis for one of the tourist niches in Tasmania today. On a lighter note, Tasmania is also well known to Westerners as the home of the 'Tasmanian Devil', made famous through the cartoons of the Walt Disney Studios. Neither of these, however, provides a valid sense of what the island is like. They do not imply natural beauty and solitude but rather harness and savagery. Thus, while the island may have a high superficial awareness, it does not enjoy wide ranging awareness of a substantive nature.

Tourism in Tasmania is not a recent phenomena. Like many island destinations with colonial histories, Tasmania has been a tourist destination for much of its history since the beginning of European settlement in the early 19th century. By the 1850s, wealthy visitors from the Australian mainland were taking advantage of the improved transportation links to Tasmania to vacation on the island. The main attractions for these early tourists were the temperate climate, the island's 'Englishness' and its natural beauty. In addition, there is evidence that the tourists, and increasingly residents, came by the 1870s to appreciate Tasmanian history and to recognize that activities could be developed that capitalized on the recent past.

This is similar pattern of tourism development to that experienced in Bermuda, although without the added attraction of having been a penal colony. In all these cases, the tourists were mostly wealthy, a necessary characteristic given the expense of reaching these island destinations and the cost of staying temporarily on them.

Tasmanian tourism must be viewed within the context of the Australian tourist sector. Although an island, Tasmania is first and foremost a state of the Commonwealth of Australia and because of this and its geographical location, it is subject to the market forces which shape Australia's tourism industry generally. There is no evidence to suggest that Tasmania is widely viewed either domestically or internationally as a destination separate and unique from Australia. Tasmanian tourism is affected to some extent by issues of transportation, cost, and by its climate and topography and this comes out in the data referred to in this section.

This does raise the question as to whether Tasmanian tourism can be positioned as a separate and unique product, distinct from Australian tourism generally. On the one hand, its location and resources suggest that creating a separate market position is not feasible. However, given the advantages which the state has in terms of niche market opportunities, policy makers and developers should consider this opportunity from a more global perspective.

Baum has identified a number of 'tourism fascination factors' which he applies to the islands in the North Atlantic.

— remoteness

— small, discrete size

— across the sea but not too far

— different but familiar

— slower pace, back a bit in time

— common heritage

— distinct culture and language

— wilderness environment

— water-focused society

— distinctive niche attractions.

All of these factors apply in varying degrees to Tasmania from the perspective of its principal tourist sources, namely Australia, Japan, North America and Europe. With this set of positive attributes, the opportunity to reposition Tasmania as an island destination within the global marketplace has some basis for optimism.

Australian tourism is characterized by the dominance of its domestic sector. While a lot of attention has been paid to the growth of international tourism in Australia, the industry is heavily dominated by domestic tourism.

The Tourism Council Australia estimates that 75% of all tourism in Australia is domestic. Growth in the sector has been relatively flat over the past 20 years with average annual growth of less than 2 per cent. Further, the Tourism Forecasting Council estimates that growth in the domestic sector will be no more than 1.4% annually through to 2007.

For the year 1999, Australians took just under 79 million overnight trips in their own country. This amounted to a total of 294.2 million overnight stays during the same period. For the period ending March 1998, the number of overnight trips was 66.3 million for a total of 262.3 million overnight stays.

Tasmania enjoys domestic overnight visits roughly comparable to its ranking in terms of population. The data also indicates that the number of domestic trips is increasing. Data for 1999, however, suggests that domestic trips fell approximately 11%. Given changes in the collection and analysis of data, accurate comparisons are not possible. Regardless, it appears that Tasmanian domestic tourism is in line with past trends and relative to the rest of Australia.

Approximately 75% of domestic tourism in Tasmania is intrastate. This is also roughly comparable to the rest of Australia. Tasmania does rank first in terms of the number of trips taken which are for pleasure or holidays. Visits to friends and relatives is comparable to other states and territories. Tasmania also ranks high in terms of domestic visit duration. In 1998, 30% of all trips in Tasmania were of 8-14 nights, the highest in Australia. Indeed, this is the highest category of visit, followed by visits of 3 nights at 19%. Data does not suggest any great variation from the rest of Australia in terms of the gender and age of domestic tourists to Tasmania. There is a higher number of intrastate domestic trips made by people in the lowest income bracket for 1998, ie under $10,000.

International tourism to Australia has generally been the success story of the 1990s. With the exception of the downturn in 1998 attributed in the main to the so called Asian economic crisis, international visitors to Australia over the past 10 years have increased, and in most cases substantially, each year. Indeed, the number of arrivals in 1999 more than doubled the total in 1990.

Clearly, Tasmania's share of the international visitor market to Australia is significantly lower than other states and territories. Tasmania ranks dead last with less than 100,000 international visitors in the period.

Tourism Strategy

Over the past several years, the development of tourism strategy in Tasmania has been the responsibility of Tourism Tasmania. This body was created in 1997 and has as its Statement of Corporate Intent, the development of "A vibrant, prosperous Tasmania where tourism is the major wealth generator". Clearly, the policy makers see the tourism sector as the primary growth area for the state in the future. Given the potential for environmental degradation as a result of rampant growth, this statement should raise some level of concern.

The agency's Mission Statement does not provide any real comfort in this regard.

> We will provide leadership in promoting Tasmania as a quality travel destination through innovative strategic marketing and sustainable development. We will achieve this in partnership with the tourism industry to maximize the economic and social benefits for all Tasmanians.
>
> Given the basis of Tasmania's appeal in the tourism marketplace, a clearer and stronger commitment to sustainable development and protection of the environment might have been expected. It is noteworthy that in the entire organization, there is no department specifically charged with monitoring the agency's activities from an environmental perspective.
>
> These stated objectives and mission are an improvement over the former tourism mission statement of the Department of Tourism, Sport and Recreation.
>
> To maximize tourism numbers, tourism expenditures, jobs, investment and development by fostering a sustainable tourism industry with potential to add substantially to economic growth.

This mission statement has all the characteristics described above by Butler where the emphasis in on sustaining tourism and not on tourism which sustains development.

The Values which the agency professes are also heavily oriented towards market forces and activity.

— shared commitment to excellence, innovation and creativity

— measuring and improving performance in pursuit of market focused objectives

— fostering individual professionalism, health and safety

— the trust and resources placed in us by Government, industry partners and the community

— being socially responsible, ethical and fair in all our relationships

— communicating openly with all out stakeholders

— Tasmania's unique environment and distinct competitive advantage.

Significant attention has been placed in the agency's business plan, Tourism 21, to enhancing the appeal of Tasmania, increasing visitations and expenditure through:

— the building of linkages with the wholesale travel market

— the design and marketing of package holidays

— consultation with the transport industry to improve access to the island

— the enhancement of international marketing activity

— the use of research to identify marketing opportunities and trends

— adoption and enhancement of electronic marketing including the development of a new web site

— building a private and public sector partnership to promote Brand Tasmania

— and strategies designed to allow Tasmania to obtain economic benefit from the Sydney Olympics

Tourism strategy is primarily focused on increasing visitor arrivals and expenditure. The agency clearly sees marketing as the principal activity with which to accomplish these objectives. The challenge is for Tourism Tasmania to attract more visitors who spend more without any negative impact on the social and natural fabric of the island. In this regard, Tasmania truly has some special advantages.

National Parks and Other Reserves

Tasmania enjoys a significant advantage with respect to the development of its parks, reserves, maritime reserves and historical sites. The development of parks and allied holdings has contributed to the current state of ecological conservation and management on the island. Almost 30% of the island is set aside as reserves of various kinds totaling 2,046,373 hectares. These reserves are managed by the Tasmania Parks and Wildlife Service (TPWS) under the National Parks and Wildlife Act 1970.

Reserves fall into nine categories including:

Type	*No*	*Size (h)*	*%*	*discription*
National Parks	18	1,424,065	20.84	large natural area of land containing a representative or outstanding sample of major natural regions, features or scenery
State Reserves	51	19,459	.28	an area of land containing significant natural landscapes or natural features; and/or sites, objects or places of significance to Aboriginal people
Nature Reserves	55	45,433	.66	an area of land that contains natural values that contribute to the natural biological diversity or geological diversity of the area of land, or both; and are unique, important or have representative value
Game Reserves	11	11,634	.17	an area of land containing natural values that are unique, important or have representative value particularly with respect to game species
Conservation Areas	123	486,968	7.12	an area of land predominantly in a natural state but mining, and in some cases, hunting, may be permitted
Nature Recre-ational Areas	14	4,064	.06	an area of land predominantly in a natural state; or containing

				sensitive natural sites of significance for recreation
Regional Reserves	3	30,850	.45	an area of land with high mineral potential or prospectivity; and predominantly in a natural state
Historic Sites	26	15,952	.023	an area of land of significance for historic cultural heritage
Private Sanctuaries	27	7,948	.012	an area of freehold land where the owner has agreed to the protection of significant natural and/or cultural values

The management objectives for all reserves recognizes fundamental issues of conservation, biodiversity and culture and tend to differ only with respect to the specific purposes of the different categories. The management objectives for the National Parks is indicative of the approach taken by the TPWS

— to conserve natural biological diversity;

— to conserve geological diversity;

— to preserve the quality of water and protect catchments;

— to conserve sites or areas of cultural significance;

— to encourage education based on the purpose of reservation and the natural or cultural values of the national park, or both;

— to encourage research, particularly that which furthers the purpose of reservation;

— to protect the national park against, and rehabilitate the national park following, adverse impacts such as those of fire, introduced species, diseases and soil erosion on the national park's natural and cultural values and on assets within and adjacent to the national park;

— to encourage and provide for tourism, recreational use and enjoyment consistent with the conservation of the national park's natural and cultural values;

— to encourage cooperative management programs with Aboriginal people in areas of significance to them in a manner consistent with the purpose of reservation and the other management objectives;

— to preserve the natural, primitive and remote character of wilderness areas.

Tourism is considered important but does not appear to be the overriding aspect of park management.

World Heritage Areas

Australia has 13 World Heritage Areas (WHA) including 2 in Tasmania: the Tasmanian Wilderness and Macquarie Island. The Tasmanian Wilderness WHA is quite special in that it is only one of 13 WHAs globally that meets all the natural criteria for selection. It is only one of 20 areas which satisfy both natural and cultural criteria. In total, it meets seven out of the 11 selection criteria. The only other WHA that meets as many criteria is Mt Taishan in China.

The Area incorporates four national parks: Walls of Jerusalem; Cradle Mountain-Lake St Clair; Southwest; and Franklin-Lower Gordon Wild Rivers). It also includes three state reserves, three forest reserves, four conservation areas, several archaeological sites as well as Macquarie Harbor. In total, the Area is approximately 1,383,640 hectares and covers some 20% of the Tasmanian island. The Area is used for the generation of hydroelectric power, and there is limited mining allowed in one conservation area.

Management of the wilderness area is through the Tasmanian Wilderness World Heritage Area Management

Plan 1999. The Plan was implemented following 2 ½ years of consultation with stakeholders and the public. Funding for the Plan comes through joint arrangements between the Commonwealth and State Governments. Overall management responsibility lies with the TPWS.

On December 3, 1997 Macquarie Island was listed as a World Heritage Area. Macquarie Island is located some 1,500 kilometres south east of Tasmania and is an Australian sub-Antarctic possession. The island is a State Reserve and has recently seen the creation of a Marine Reserve. Access to the Island has been restricted since 1979 and is by permit only. The Island is an example of the progressive approach which Tasmania has taken toward the preservation of its natural assets. It was declared a wildlife sanctuary in 1933 and became a State Reserve in 1972. In 1977, it became an IUCN Biosphere Reserve and is the only one in the Southern Ocean. In 1997, it became Tasmania's second World Heritage Area.

The parks and reserves provide a range of activities upon which tourism depends including hang gliding, abseiling, rockclimbing, caving, limited hunting, some four wheel drives, and some horseriding.

Bush walking is a major activity with the Wilderness Heritage Area offering over 1000 kilometres of walking track including the Overland Track, Frenchman's Cap Track, Port Davey Track, and the South Coast Track. These tracks alone allow hikers to cover most of the southern and middle regions of Tasmania in pristine wilderness settings. Usage is increasing and the TPWS estimates that over 20,000 visits occur annually with less traveled trails becoming more popular. In response, the TPWS has developed a Walking Track Management Strategy designed to minimize the impact of visitors.

The Tasmanian Trail extends from Devonport on the northern shore of the island 480 kilometres to Dover on the south coast. The trail is multi-purpose and allows for hiking, mountain biking and horse riding. It is composed of existing forest tracks and fire trails, roads and some trails over private land. Because it is multi-purpose, it relieves some of the pressure on conventional hiking trails in the national parks which are confined strictly to hikers. The Trail provides a somewhat different experience than bushwalking in that it offers a wider range of accommodation and activities.

Rafting and boating is allowed on a number of the rivers in the national parks including the Franklin and Gordon. There is concern about the level of shoreline erosion on both rivers and particularly in the Gordon. TPWS regularly monitors erosion. As part of its effort to limit damage, it has developed with the West Coast Community Council, the Gordon River Boating Code which sets outs rules and guidelines for users of the river. The Code has been in effect since 1992.

Boating has also increased the usage of other parts of the Wilderness area including Bathurst Harbor and Port Davey on the southwest corner of the park. TPWS estimate that usage has increased 500% over the past decade, due in part to more accurate charts, GPS's, organized cruises and the increased use of light aircraft. In order to control the impact of the increased usage, a range of regulations and guidelines have been developed to control the movement of boats, the number of sites for landing, the disposal of waste and in some parts of the region, access by boats.

In addition to boating, other forms of sea based activity is available through the national parks including sea kayaking, canoeing, sailing and angling.

Tasmania also has a number of Marine Reserves along the east coast of the island including Governor Island, Maria Island, Ninepin Point, and Tinderbox Marine Reserve. In 2000, a Marine Reserve was also proclaimed on Macquarie Island. Policy for the management of the marine reserves is being developed by the Marine and Marine Industries Council established by the Minister for Primary Industries, Water and Environment in 1999. The Council consists of 18 members representing various stakeholders and expertise in the use, management and conservation of marine areas. The Council has produced a draft strategy designed to identify and establish reserves and is currently inviting comment from the community at large on the draft.

Approximately 100,000 people annually take cruises on Macquarie Harbor and the Lower Gordon River embarking from the village of Strahan. This level of traffic impacts on the Gordon River. In addition to erosion concerns, other threats to the Wilderness Area include erosion on the Central Plateau area, degradation in caves and trails, plant disease infestation and the introduction of non-indigenous species of plants and animals.

There are six properties designated as Wilderness Lodges, including the internationally known Cradle Mountain Lodge and the Freycinet Lodge. They are the principal accommodation within Tasmania's national parks and are managed in accordance with environmentally sound hotel management practices.

Freycinet Lodge is located on the Freycinet Peninsula some 200 kilometres north of Hobart on Tasmania's east coast. It consists of 21 apartments and 39 rooms for a total capacity of 285 persons. The Lodge also provides a small conference facility. Its public areas are fairly upmarket but the design and construction of all buildings results in minimal impact on the surrounding area.

Cradle Mountain Lodge is similar to the Freycinet Lodge in that it provides accommodation mainly in standalone cabins with a central public area. Capacity at the Lodge is 356 persons and it also has limited conference facilities. it is located near to the entrance of Cradle Mountain Park. Also in the region is the Cradle Country Chalet with a capacity of 16 persons.

Other Wilderness Lodges include the Central Highlands Lodge with a capacity of 20 persons specializing in trout fishing, the Lemonthyme Lodge with a capacity of 92 persons, and the Silver Ridge Retreat with a capacity of 50 persons.

Convict Tourism

The irony for Tasmania is that the very activity which brought the island such infamy in the 19th century has provided the foundation for a unique and successful niche form of tourism. More so than any other destination, Tasmania has a range of historical sights emanating from the period in its history when it was considered to be the place where England transported its worst criminals.

Tourists to Tasmania have long been fascinated by the penal history of the island. This early interest is now dwarfed by the level of interest which contemporary tourists to Tasmania demonstrate. This interest has led to increases in tourist activity on the West Coast in Macquarie Harbor and the Village of Strahan through the development of the Sarah Island site. Most telling is the fact that the Port Arthur Historical Site is now the most visited tourist attraction in Tasmania. In 1998, 45% of all international visitors to Tasmania visited the Port Arthur Site compared with Freycinet National Park (17%) and Cradle Mountain National Park (28%). Of the 26 historic sites, eight are significant because of their role in the penal system: Coal Mines (Tasman Peninsula); Eaglehawk Neck (Tasman Peninsula); Female Factory (Hobart); Macquarie Harbor; Old Trinity Church-Criminal Courts (Hobart); Port Arthur; Richmond Goal; and the Ross Female Convict Station.

In addition to the major tourism attractions discussed above, Tasmania is also developing niche markets in a number of areas which build upon the strengths of the island, particularly in the area of agriculture. The island offers a range of agricultural based tourist activities including farm stays, agricultural museums, and specialist centers focusing on particular crops such as lavender and raspberries. Wine tourism in Tasmania is increasing along with the general growth in the wine industry in Australia and in Tasmania particularly.

As is the case with many of Australia's tourism destinations, the development of events are an important part of Tasmanian tourism. The two major events are the Sydney to Hobart Yacht Race held over the Christmas holidays and the Targa Tasmania rally.

5

Challenges of Island Tourism

After decades of immense development, by the year 2005 tourism will be among the world's largest industries. Its enormous growth brings with it tremendous benefits, but also considerable threats to the environment in its broad sense, including the natural, social and built environment. Many deficits in the field of tourism such as the lack of standardization of definitions, market research and planning, adequate policies and legislation, information on tourism's possible implications and cooperation between key players have been aggravated by exponential and often uncontrolled growth.

In the past 40 years, international tourism has grown rapidly; from 1950 when 25 million tourists generated ECU8 billion in receipts, to 1990 when around 460 million tourists generated ECU260 billion. In addition it is estimated that there are almost three times as many domestic tourists. Tourism is today the world's largest employer, employing 212 million people worldwide, that is, one in every nine jobs. In the EU it employs 7 million people and accounts for over 5 per cent of Gross Domestic Product and foreign trade.

According to the World Travel & Tourism Council (WTTC), between 1995 and 2005, Travel & Tourism will:

- Double in size in nominal terms
- Increase its output by more than 50 per cent in real terms
- Add one new job every 2.5 seconds
- Create 125 million new direct and indirect jobs

However, besides the opportunities to be gained with tourism development, such as job and income generation, there has also been a significant increase in the threats and conflicts arising from its often uncontrolled growth. Tourism was once perceived as a clean, non-resource-consumptive economic activity, free of the environmental impacts attributed to manufacturing, mining and intensive agriculture. Since the 1970s this benign view of tourism has been increasingly questioned.

In order for tourism to carry on flourishing the resources which it uses intensively must continue to be available (i.e. pristine landscapes and coastline, unpolluted seas, and so on). This highlights the value of nature for tourism –beyond its intrinsic value. The negative consequences of high-volume tourism can be summarized in two main effects: massive usage of resources (water, energy, soil, landscape, etc.) and massive emissions (waste, wastewater, noise, air emissions, etc.).

Today environmental compatibility is high on the list of essentials for holiday locations. Tour operators are asked to offer unspoiled landscape and nature. By exceeding carrying capacities on the physical, social and ecological levels, tourism is destroying its own basis and is endangering its own long-term future.

In Europe, the impacts of tourism are exacerbated by the concentration of tourist activities into a short holiday season and relatively small areas. Much of the damage done to the environment as a result of tourism is caused by the pressure of the volume of visitors arriving at destinations which are not used to supporting people in such great numbers. Growth in visitor numbers also puts severe strain on the local capacity of specific geographical areas such as coastal areas, mountains and wetlands. Wetlands for example are among the world's most threatened and exploited habitats. The rate of their destruction has been very rapid in the last 40 years, particularly in the Mediterranean basin and in coastal regions.

A tourist boom can also have a significant impact on the local community. While communities often want the benefits of tourism, they may often lack a realistic understanding of what is involved in achieving this development and the likely impacts of tourism. The influx of tourists on small islands for example is often highly seasonal with a dramatic peak in the summer. During this period, visitors often outnumber the native population, which puts undoubted pressures on the local culture and resources. Concerns amongst the island population about how to handle large tourist numbers, how to distribute economic benefits and about the future of tourism are frequent.

At the same time the economic importance of tourism for islands must be recognized. Tourism is often vitally important in sustaining the population. Consequently the issues of how to manage tourism are complex.

Despite these issues, measures aiming at tackling (adverse) tourism impact have only slowly emerged and most are either fragmentary and/or remain at a theoretical level. This is to be observed with regard to many legal as well as voluntary approaches which show shortcomings in the form of a lack of commitment to objectives, action and deadlines, aggravated by the insufficient involvement and participation of many actors.

Managerial measures, drawn up by management staff of areas exposed to increased tourism influx, are mostly tailor-made for areas limited in space and scope. As there is barely any exchange of experience or consultation taking place amongst the key players involved, other areas are unable to benefit from experiences made at, ideally, reduced cost.

The challenges that islands faces and their future options has become a matter for intense discussion in recent years. The subject of islands started to appear in the international community in 1992, when Agenda 21 that came out of the Rio Conference unequivocally stated that islands represent an essential part in the world wide strategy of sustainable development. Chapter 17 of Agenda 21 points out that "islands constitute a special case, both for the environment and for development, and they present very specific problems in the planning of sustainable development. They tend to be ecologically fragile and vulnerable." On the other hand, their small individual size, their limited resources, geographical dispersion and their isolation from markets place them at an economic disadvantage and prevent them from achieving economies of scale.

The Barbados Conference, in its preamble, also provided a common attitude, recognition of the force of insularity in the international community: "we see that, although, when considered individually, islands and small island states cover a small surface area, collectively they exercise jurisdiction over a sixth of the Earth's surface area". And this is without counting the influence of the thousands of other islands that are administratively dependent on mainland states. A peculiarity that is clearly illustrated in the case of Vanuatu, an archipelago of eighty islands with a land area that is fifty times less than its exclusive economic area (600,000 km^2), with a population of 150,000 inhabitants.

The appearance of a new mentality and the building of the island conscience in the dawn of the XXI century have a common link; the fact that island societies have become aware that the wealth and diversity of the natural heritage of islands is seriously endangered, and that safeguard strategies for this heritage should be designed on specific budgets. This is nothing new.

The colonisation of island territories on the basis of hyper-specialised production superimposed on the land is a common practice, and has been for over three hundred years. This is the case of sugar cane introduction, which created the White Gold Route from Cape Verde to the West Indies, tea as a single crop, or the introduction on a massive scale of bananas in Madeira, the Canary Islands, the West Indies or Madagascar. In many cases, this specialisation has radically altered fragile island ecosystems.

Now however, a new single crop has exploded onto the scene with unusual force, before the eyes of island peoples; tourism. This is an ambivalent phenomenon that provides the resources that island economies need, but which has a capacity of land occupation and competition that could have totally unpredictable effects. If we analyse the international arrivals data supplied by the WTO (World Tourism Organisation), islands, as a whole, can be considered the world's second leading tourist destination, behind the block formed by historic cities.

But, getting a close up view of the reality of the island situation, especially in tourist matters, is a task that is absolutely obscured by an accumulation of curious historic perceptions. The extreme diversity of islands has turned them into unknown territory, as a whole, surrounded by myths and sometimes standardised, a perception that includes the tourist expectations created in recent decades for island destinations.

In the eyes of many mainlanders, we see that their vision of islands remains impregnated with this age-old mix of fantasy and ignorance. Like the islands of the Odyssey, those small worlds that Ulysses found before reaching Ithaca. Let us not forget that as imaginary territories, islands have been the sites of great utopias like the Atlantis evoked by Plato in two of his Dialogues, or the most insular of utopias represented in Francis' Bacon's New Atlantis. On the other end of the scale from the utopia is the desert island, described by Alphonse Daudet in his Shipwreck, or by Jules Verne, in his Mysterious Island, islands of fear or punishment, as Unamuno reminds us when he refers to Fuerteventura, or infamous islands or prison islands, like Gorée.

The XIX century brought the discovery of islands as the perfect dreams of naturalists, a sanctuary for what we now understand as biodiversity. They are the islands of Linus and Rousseau, islands that coined Darwin's evolution of the species. That is why, nowadays, island expectations are forged with a tremendous amount of real capital based on diversity and that indefinable cultural, scenic and social mix that, in each specific case, defines thousands of singular islands. These reflections are key elements in the analysis of the emerging role of islands in the international tourist market.

In the times we live in, however, there is confrontation between islands in new competitivity scenarios of the tourist industry. For the present mature island destinations, aspects related to environmental and cultural quality are not optional added values, they now constitute essential specifications of the product that will decide its level of survival in the market.

The Ecomost project, carried out in 1994 for the islands of Rhodes and Majorca, gave us a foretaste of the basic problems that island tourist destinations are now facing when it stated that any destination that is irreversibly damaged in its basic environmental aspects, will pay the price of ail products that become uncompetitive. Eco-tourist quality is appearing as an objective to pursue in destinations like islands. But, apart from these market driven reactions and an increasingly aware demand, it is essential to recognise that the context of tourist activity is now changing at a dizzying speed. Tourism has fundamentally changed its dimension, as a mass phenomenon and even as a social right, a change that also includes the forms, with the systematic appearance of new products, destinations and ways of understanding the art of travelling.

The tourist business in islands has also changed to the same extent. Tourism was initially managed by the owners of the accommodation in the destination; then tour operators appeared and carriers, and, more recently, there has been a broad process of merger between the latter and the major accommodation chains. But, if we analyse the new century, once again we would stress another major change. If we really look carefully at what we have so far understood as conventional tourism, we see this is a mere fraction of the great leisure industry.

Apart from the obvious evidence like the Disney phenomenon, the international reorganisation of the industry in the context of the global market clearly points to this trend. In fact, tourism forecasting now has to be done in the framework of the Information Society. In the age of telematics, and within a very few years, it will be very difficult to recognise the conventional forms and products that have characterised the tourist business so far.

These changes must be observed with special attention by islands in order to anticipate what sometimes appear to be irreversible events. An approach is required that is based on the fact that the penetration of tourism in new island economies constitutes an increasingly determining factor in their future strategy. For reference information, one only has to emphasise that this sector represents a growing proportion of the Gross National Product of a larger and larger number of island regions, with varying degrees of intensity, like the cases of Okinawa (20%), Hawaii (56%), Northern Mariana Islands (67%), The Canary Islands (60%). The trend towards specialisation becomes more evident if we analyse data such as the weight of employment in the tertiary sector: Reunion (77%), the Canary Islands (80%).

To get an idea of the importance of island tourism, if we compare usual island tourist densities within the European Union we find densities reaching 150 beds per square kilometre, higher in many cases than the density in many populated areas of the continent. But in terms of tourist flows, the results are a lot more striking: Greek islands receive more international tourism than Brazil, the Balearic Islands host as many tourist as Portugal and the Canary Islands doubles the 6 million international tourists received by South Africa, the great emerging destination. In this context, the experience of the seven Canary Islands represents an excellent expression of the paradigm of tourism in islands. Many different forms of tourist development and different design policies live together in a very limited space of land.

Issues of Climate Change and Natural Disasters

The UN Secretary-General emphasizes that climate change and sea-level rise can inflict serious economic damage on many small islands, particularly in highly developed coastal areas where buildings and infrastructure for tourism, fisheries and other important economic activities are located.

Regarding natural disasters, the Secretary-General mentions that, since the adoption of the Programme of Action, small island nations have collectively been forced to face "the unpredictability, frequency and intensity" of numerous extreme weather events each year. "Because of the consequent diversion of resources from long-term development plans to deal with reconstruction and rehabilitation, natural disasters continue to pose a formidable challenge to sustainable development for most of them," the report states.

"Climate change and sea level rise" is the first item in the Barbados Programme of Action. At the national level, most of the small island States have strengthened their response to climate change by initiating arrangements to establish permanent national climate change focal points within their Governments. They have ratified the Kyoto Protocol on climate change, which was approved a few years later, and for which SIDS are calling for immediate entry into force.

To provide better forecasts, with the help of the World Meteorological Organization (WMO), small islands have upgraded their data collection systems that enable them to collect, analyse and interpret meteorological data. Although contingency planning and response preparedness in SIDS remain fairly weak at the national level, this has been alleviated to some extent by regional initiatives.

Twelve countries have engaged in Caribbean Planning for Adaptation to Climate Change, a project designed to support the participating countries in preparing to cope with the adverse effects of global climate change, particularly sea-level rise in coastal and marine areas. Some areas of concern remained, though, namely vulnerability assessment, adaptation planning and related capacity building. A second phase called Mainstreaming Adaptation to Climate Change is currently being conducted to facilitate an enabling environment for climate change.

Small island States are deeply concerned that the world's collective failure so far to reduce greenhouse emissions has increased their vulnerability, and they would like to be better supported to adapt and protect themselves. In his report, the Secretary-General stresses the importance of adaptation to climate change, disaster preparedness and risk management, and calls for integrated planning and decision-making on coastal zone management, fisheries, agriculture, tourism, energy, health and water resource management. "Crucially, the international community needs to redouble efforts to put in place an effective regime to deal with climate change and its consequences," he states.

Freshwater Resources Management

On volcanic and atoll islands, surface and groundwater resources are limited. Elsewhere, when the nature of the soil is not an issue, freshwater supplies have continued to be polluted and demand has increased due to urbanization. However, the situation of small island nations varies widely. While some face food security challenges because of poor soil quality, the smaller islands and the atolls are practically self-sufficient. Small islands still face deficiencies in water availability, water catchments and storage, pollution of water resources, saline intrusion and leakage in the delivery system.

While there has been significant development in the area of freshwater resources, notes the Secretary-General in his report, watershed management in many small island developing States is still weak, because of the inadequacy of technical equipment, trained technicians, data on groundwater systems, watershed planning and management systems. "This has resulted in the inadequate monitoring of the supply and quality of freshwater," he notes. The report mentions that some islands have seen increases in gastrointestinal illness, in particular among children, as a result of water being polluted by untreated sewage. Untreated waste water discharged into coastal waters has contributed significantly to damaging coastal ecosystems and coral reefs.

Already scarce, land resources are further subjected to competing demands by population pressure, deforestation and soil erosion. The scarcity of land affects waste management as well. Population growth and the development of tourism generate more waste while there are simply not enough disposal sites. The pressure that existed ten years ago on land resources has since been further exacerbated.

Over the last decade, some water management technologies have been tested successfully in some islands. For instance, a new "scavenger" technology for wells, introduced in the Marshall Islands with assistance from the

United Nations and the North American National Weather Service (NOAA), is an inexpensive, practical solution for controlling saltwater intrusion when groundwater is drawn. As a result of the Barbados Programme of Action, some small island countries have made significant progress in dealing with domestic waste management issues, while most are still lacking financial and technical capacity.

In some small island developing States, the private sector has become involved in recycling biodegradable and non-biodegradable materials, such as paper, plastics, metal cans and used oil. Economic incentives to reduce wastes, such as a deposit refund system for cans and bottles, have been introduced and are in use in virtually all regions. However, small islands have expressed a growing concern with regard to the security and environmental implications of the disposal and transport of radioactive materials and the lack of liability and compensation regimes.

The Secretary-General calls for more effective legislation, management and enforcement measures with respect to freshwater resources, sanitation and waste, and encourages improved tracking and management of the movement and disposal of hazardous and toxic substances to ensure the protection of the fragile marine ecosystems of SIDS. He also welcomes financial, technical and technological support for the development of appropriate waste management systems in small island developing States.

Managing Transport and Energy Sector

"Tourism and its contribution to the economies of small island developing States are threatened by overdevelopment, pollution, loss of biodiversity, climate change, beach erosion, social and cultural conflict, crime and, more recently, the threat of terrorism," the Secretary-General says in his report. Tourism, which remains a principal economic activity for most SIDS, increased by about 60 per cent during the 1990s. Negatively affected after the terrorist attack of September 2001, this sector is now recovering.

Small islands have traditionally depended and still rely on imports of petroleum products for much of their energy needs, especially for transportation and electricity generation. Because many remote and rural areas have little or no access to modern and affordable energy, they often turn to fuelwood, thus contributing to deforestation. The cost of electricity generation is relatively high because of transportation costs, small-scale generating systems and low-density, scattered populations. The high cost of power is an obstacle to foreign investment, and represents for most islands a significant proportion of import costs.

Isolated and distant from the mainland, the small islands lack adequate international and domestic transport facilities and services. Transport and communications networks are often fragmented and costly, due to monopoly service providers. They are generally poorly developed and maintained. Furthermore, security requirements to counter terrorism have introduced financial demands that add to already high transport costs for many islands.

The Secretary-General, in his report, acknowledges the important steps being taken by many small islands, at the national and regional level, to strengthen tourism planning and management so as to include environmental concerns and maximize social and economic benefits. These include the establishment of land use standards for tourism development, integrated watershed and coastal area management systems and approaches.

For instance, five Caribbean nations launched in 2003 the eco-tourism "Blue Flag Caribbean pilot project" with the goal of improving water quality and enhancing environmental education and management in tourism operations. The Secretary-General also encourages the island nations to ensure that tourism development "is pursued within the context of an integrated development plan that is cognizant of social considerations and environmental management requirements."

Many islands have developed or are developing hydropower, geothermal, solar and wind power, and biomass energy, in some cases through private-public partnerships. In a number of islands, small-scale solar photovoltaic (PV) power systems have been used to provide electricity in rural and remote areas on a pilot scale. The Secretary-General's report calls for more seed funding and energy investments to address the energy vulnerability of small island developing States, improve their energy efficiency at all levels and develop renewable energy resources.

Managing Marine Resources

Many small island developing States, including the Dominican Republic, Fiji, Haiti, Jamaica and Mauritius, have a high percentage of unique and diverse animal and plant species. The ecosystems of many islands are small and vulnerable to disruption by climate change or other human activities. SIDS therefore have many rare, endangered and threatened species. Population growth and development, natural disasters and the introduction of alien species threaten biodiversity.

Fisheries and other marine resources are economically critical in many islands, providing a large share of the food supply, employment, economic activity and income. These resources are threatened by overexploitation, destructive harvesting, land-based pollution, pollution from ships, coastal development, climate change and invasive alien species. The greatest threat to the coastal and marine environment comes from land-based sources of pollution, including human wastes, industrial effluent and agricultural run-off. If they are not properly managed, fishing industries and tourism can also deteriorate and deplete the resources on which those very communities depend.

Unfortunately the ability of SIDS to fully and effectively manage coastal and marine resources in a sustainable manner varies greatly. Most island Governments lack the resources and capacity for effective national surveillance and monitoring. Coralreefs are particularly rich marine ecosystems that are currently under threat. SIDS also report that bio-prospecting and bio-piracy continue to rise.

All SIDS are parties to the Convention on Biological Diversity and most have taken advantage ofopportunities to develop national biodiversity strategies initiating national strategic action plans and developing national nature reserves and protected areas. Financial and other resource constraints, however, have undermined their efforts to implement these strategies. A major source of support for protecting biodiversity in SIDS has been Global Environment Facility (GEF), especially through its role as financial mechanism for the Convention on Biological Diversity.

To implement the Barbados Programme of Action, the Food and Agricultural Organization of the United Nations (FAO) has provided technical assistance to SIDS totalling

$90 million, for 520 field projects in 38 countries. Twenty-one small island nations have signed the International Plant Protection Convention (IPPC), which aims to prevent the introduction of pests affecting plants and plant products and to promote measures for their control. SIDS have recorded significant progress in regional cooperation in the area of fisheries, notably through the establishment of legal regimes.

In his report, the Secretary-General suggests that more attention be devoted to the protection of small islands' traditional knowledge relating to biodiversity, since there are no accepted international standards to accord intellectual property rights to communities. He expresses hope that islanders could be supported in making more productive use of their biological diversity to generate resources for development.

On marine resources, the Secretary-General notes progress in regional cooperation on fisheries, including through the establishment of legal regimes. The report mentions that international support has focused on specific areas such as fish stocks assessment, ocean observation and monitoring, and direct payments for fishery licences.

Challenges in Recycling

Island recycling is far more complex than recycling anywhere on the mainland. There are two particularly significant reasons: the lack of local – or even regional – markets for recyclables, and the cost of shipping materials inter-island as well as to off-island markets.

Successful recycling depends on manufacturing, and no where else is this precept more obvious than in an island economy which supports no manufacturing. Productive manufacturing – which is based on profit realized on sales of goods manufactured – relies on easy access to cheap raw materials. But "easy access to" and "cheap" are two phrases usually not associated with island life. Without an already-established industrialized base, island economies find it difficult to start up manufacturing or recycling companies. Additionally, most island governments have traditionally supported the visitor industries, since the tourist dollar usually has a more immediate return-on-investment than a manufacturing dollar. For example, if you spend a dollar buying a souvenir trinket, that dollar is returned immediately to the local economy through the retail establishment or street vendor. This vendor will then pass a percentage of the dollar to the distributor, the wholesaler and ultimately the manufacturer.

In island economies however, these "uplink" businesses are almost always located off-island. Because of the nature of manufacturing and international trade, retail establishments usually represent lost opportunity costs. Most often the only local jobs they support are in the companies that service their businesses, which traditionally pay less than manufacturing jobs.

On the other hand, economic returns from manufacturing operations almost always support multiple layers of a local economy, but the return on investment is more subtle and less immediate. In recycling, for example, a re-manufacturing company will support jobs in the local collection and processing companies in addition to the jobs created within its own operations. Additionally, the value added to the end product through the manufacturing process will be realized with additional taxes paid to the local economy, either through employment, sales, or other operations. The multiplier effect of every dollar is higher in the manufacturing trades than in retail.

Tourism however, is usually considered a "clean" industry, while manufacturing has traditionally been viewed as "dirty". Since island economies rely on visitor dollars, they are very concerned with maintaining beauty and image. Individuals and companies that choose to work in recycling collection, processing and re-manufacturing in an island economy face similar but more complex challenges than their mainland counterparts. In most island economies, recycling is an anomaly and knowledge of the recycling industry is limited among business developers and financing institutions. This lack of familiarity, accompanied by a few failures over the decades makes it extremely difficult for a business to obtain funds to start-up or expand operations. The financiers are not confident that the money invested can be recovered by local resale of machinery and equipment, should the business fail.

As a result, most successful collection and processing companies are started small, with second-hand equipment and a focus on two or three materials. This helps to protect the companies from over-capitalizing and taking on too much debt that will sink their ships when markets inevitably collapse and transportation expenses outstrip their revenues.

Actual recycling of materials on any island is extremely rare, since so little manufacturing exists. Companies that wish to establish such operations in the islands face an almost impossible problem with their bottom lines. Their start-up costs of transporting machinery and equipment and the expense of maintenance, repair and replacement of their machinery are a significant cost and ultimate debt that may easily cause them to price their end products out of reach of the local market.

Additionally, re-manufacturing companies need to supply enough finished product at competitive rates to meet local demand. Capitalization costs alone may make it impossible to meet or beat the prices charged by large-scale manufacturers that have already fully amortized their property or have huge production runs and as a result can spread the cost of their products far more widely.

Finally, the island manufacturing company must be able to count on the local collection systems, which are often spread throughout the islands, to provide it with enough raw material to manufacture sufficient quantities of the end product to meet the demand of its markets. The collectors and processors on neighboring islands, however, may not be able to afford the costs of the inter-island transportation based on the revenues from sales to the local manufacturer.

Solid Waste Management in Hawai Island

This section discusses the challenges of solid waste management in Hawai Islands, one of the famous tourist destination of the world. The easy island lifestyle that seems so exciting is completely dependent upon the importation of just about everything. Hawaii, for example, prides itself on its tourism, which is largely based on the consumption of food, drink, beach supplies, hotels, and trinkets. Ninety-nine percent of the products used to supply tourism and the residents of Hawaii are imported. Virtually nothing is manufactured from raw materials on the islands to meet the demands of its visitor industry or its resident population. As a result, state and county solid waste officials have tried a variety of measures to stem the flow of what will ultimately become the 2.1 million tons of garbage left behind each year from the 5 million tourists and 1.4 million residents. In 1990, the Hawaii Legislature approved recommendations made in the Integrated Solid Waste Management Plan developed by a committee of business people, environmentalists, regulators and county solid waste officials. The Integrated Solid Waste Management Act requires each county to develop programs to achieve 50 percent diversion of municipal solid waste by the year 2000.

The legislation established the Office of Solid Waste Management (OSWM) under the Department of Health for regulatory and planning purposes, and named the Department of Business, Economic Development & Tourism (DBEDT) responsible for recycling market development. In 1993, a group of concerned business people, legislators, county council members and environmentalists were successful in lobbying the legislature to create the Clean Hawaii Center within DBEDT to assist businesses in developing the capacity to recycle materials throughout the islands. The Center was supported by DBEDT in its initial year, but in its second year staff positions were eliminated as the state faced a severe economic crisis. Only one program of the Center continues as a result of funding from the OSWM, and that is to use a competitive bid process to distribute $250,000 to recycling businesses engaged in research and development. The administrative process however, restricted companies from using the funds to purchase machinery and equipment.

John Harder, chief of solid waste for the state of Hawaii, placed no conditions on the use of the funds by businesses and was disturbed by DBEDT's restrictions. "I am really disappointed that they restricted the use of this money, especially since it was money from our office and we were looking at alternative ways to get the money to companies," he says. In 1994, the state initiated a 25-cent-per-ton tipping fee (raised to 35 cents by the 1997 legislature) to pay for administration of its solid waste management program. Additionally, the state imposed a 1.5-cent advanced disposal fee on all glass containers entering the state. In 1996, this disposal fee resulted in the collection of $2.4 million, 90 percent of which was distributed to the counties to operate or contract for glass recycling programs.

Harder estimates that of the 2.1 million tons of MSW produced in 1996, 500,000 tons were diverted from the waste stream and recycled, recovered, or composted. Maui led the islands in recycling, with a 25 percent diversion rate; Oahu estimated 24.5 percent diversion; the Big Island of Hawaii diverted 17.5 percent; and 15 percent of Kauai's MSW was diverted. In 1993, legislation was passed to redefine recycling as a manufacturing activity rather than a solid waste disposal alternative. DBEDT argued with the OSWM that this determination should exempt companies involved in the re-manufacturing of secondary paper, plastics, and glass from having to obtain solid waste permits. DBEDT maintained that the materials collected were clean and separated prior to disposal in the waste stream, and as raw materials for a manufacturing process could not be discriminated against.

But the OSWM did not want to lose its ability to force correction of disposal abuses that might result in public health hazards. A compromise was reached where the manufacturing company could submit a simple letter for a "permit by rule" which would alert the OSWM to its activities and would allow the OSWM to track its progress and lower the hammer if violations occurred. Companies that collect or process the secondary materials – or the raw materials used by the manufacturers – are granted relaxed permitting but are still regulated under solid waste management statutes.

The island of Oahu (home to Honolulu) has a waste-to-energy facility which was erected in 1986 with a put-or-pay contract to burn 600,000 tons of MSW per year. The facility, built with bond financing at a cost of $60 million, is one of two licensed MSW disposal sites on the island. Oahu's landfill, which is operated by Waste Management Inc., has approximately four years of disposal capacity remaining. A privately owned and operated construction and demolition debris landfill receives these special wastes at a substantial cost difference from the MSW facilities.

Honolulu uses a series of 60 drop off containers, located at schools throughout the island, to collect old newspaper, glass, aluminum, and plastic milk bottles. The schools receive the money earned after expenses paid to the recycling processor. In the initial stages of the program, schools were earning $50 to $100 per container, which is collected either weekly or twice a month depending on the location. The downturn in paper prices has resulted in the revenues dropping to $1 to $5 per container.

Honolulu does its best to use the recyclables in the state. The milk bottles are shipped to Maui, where Aloha Plastics processes them for their extruded plastic lumber operations; glass is crushed and either shipped to the West Coast or mixed into glassphalt or cement. Yard trimmings will be picked up at curbside from residences that are assigned the city's new automated collection system. Honolulu also has encouraged green waste recycling with a few contracts to businesses to operate wood and green waste processing sites.

The majority of Honolulu's recovered materials come from the commercial sector. Suzanne Jones, recycling coordinator for the city and county of Honolulu, feels that material disposal bans are an effective means of stimulating diversion efforts. Trucks are monitored at the county's disposal facilities, and may not contain more than 25 percent cardboard or yard trimmings. A total disposal ban has been instituted for scrap metals, white goods, tires and batteries.

The county has legislated that all offices greater than 20,000 square feet must recycle old newspapers, office paper and cardboard. Restaurants and bars serving alcoholic beverages must recycle glass. Large food processors, food preparation operations, kitchens, grocery stores, and restaurants must recycle their food wastes. This material has traditionally been given to the island hog farmers, or collected for a fee by Unisyn, a food and animal waste processing facility that uses an anaerobic digestion process to convert it to a usable soil amendment.

Most businesses are able to comply with these mandates. "We want to keep it based on sound economics," Jones stresses. "If a company cannot meet our diversion requirements for economic reasons we will review and sometimes relax these requirements on a case-by-case basis."

Maui operates one transfer station and one central landfill that has two years of space remaining in its current phase, and an additional 20 years anticipated with phases 4 to 6. Additionally, Maui has developed a network of recycling drop-off sites, a sewage sludge/green waste composting program, and a bio-diesel project that converts used cooking grease into diesel. The island has also used grants to encourage small-scale re-manufacturing in plastics and glass. Dr. Hana Steel, Maui's recycling coordinator, credits community pride and participation for the island's successful and creative approaches to developing end-use businesses. The support of Mayor Linda Lingle, TEAM MAUI and the grassroots Maui Recycling Group have been critical for the program's successes over the past eight years.

The Big Island of Hawaii has transfer stations situated throughout the island and two licensed landfills. The Hilo site has approximately 18 months of operating life remaining, while the new Kona landfill operated by Waste Management Inc. has another 50 years of life expectancy.

The Big Island, however, was recently sued by the United Public Workers Union for privatizing services that could be provided by civil servants. The union won its lawsuit and the county has notified WMI – which won the contract in 1994 to build and operate the facility – that it will assume operation of the site within 18 months.

The island's recycling contract to Recycling Systems Hawaii was temporarily suspended during the legal action but is expected to resume shortly. The business operates commercial recycling, buy back and drop-boxes for newspaper, glass, aluminum and plastic. They crush the glass on-site using an Andela Pulverizer, and have marketed the resulting product as a soil additive, decorative glass rocks for aquariums and landscaping purposes, among various other uses. The paper, aluminum and corrugated cardboard are sold out-of-state, the plastics are sold to Aloha Plastics on Maui.

A few composting companies struggle to make ends meet on the Big Island, producing quality soil amendments from local green wastes that are brought to the sites by tree trimmers and landscapers. The Big Island does not maintain a recycling coordinator, but in the past has contracted these services through the local non-profit group, Recycle Hawaii.

Kauai's landfill, which had only three years of space remaining in 1991, was filled in one week by debris generated when Hurricane Iniki hit the island in September 1991. The island is currently using a temporary facility, which has another 18 months of capacity. Kauai has no recycling coordinator, and eliminated its solid waste manager's position in 1996. The island currently supports a scrap metal processor, a glass recycler, and a company that receives green waste for composting.

Despite all of their determination, it seems unlikely that the islands of Hawaii can reach their goal of diverting 50 percent of the waste stream annually by the end of this century. Scrap metals still represent the majority of materials diverted from each island. This is the result of aggressive efforts to reduce stockpiles of abandoned vehicles, and the demolition of military and sugar cane processing complexes.

Much of the research we conducted in the early years of the Clean Hawaii Center focused on the potential to establish small scale or niche market re-manufacturing companies that could beat the prices of imported products by using the transportation costs as the pricing cushion. For example, we knew that most products imported to Hawaii carried a transportation cost that ranged from 40 percent to 80 percent of their wholesale price. A local company could use this spread to price their products competitively and still cover higher operating costs. We also focused on micro businesses that could support the full circle from collections to manufacturing, on each island with populations ranging from 1,200 to 1.2 million.

The islands of Hawaii will always remain vulnerable to the international price wars surrounding secondary materials because it does not – and probably never will – have the capacity to absorb its own paper, metals or all of its plastics. According to research done by the Clean Hawaii Center, however, the islands have the ability to use all of its wood, green wastes, glass, and food wastes.

The OSWM is currently exploring the creation of a local chapter of the Solid Waste Association of North America, since there is no similar organization of its type in the state. In cooperation with the Rural Community Assistance Corp., the OSWM is also conducting community meetings to determine the feasibility of establishing a non-profit recyclers' association or a similar entity based on cooperatively run businesses.

The businesses that have survived, sometimes in spite of government assistance, insist that all they need is for the government to even the playing field between the assistance it provides to solid waste management and what they provide to recycling businesses. For example, the state has provided land, free of charge to the counties, on which to build existing landfills and transfer stations. If that same land were provided free of charge to the recyclers they could easily make a profit, expand collections and processing, and establish more re-manufacturing operations.

Tackling the Challenges from Tourism

In view of this, sustainable tourism development and management will not be achieved unless a new approach to tourism is taken, adopting a holistic viewpoint and sustainable practices, hence generating an equal share of the benefits and costs for all stakeholders. A new partnership between tourism, local communities and the environment is needed, including necessary changes in attitudes, behaviour, and management.

Tourism must be considered, planned and managed in a much more integrated way than it has been to date, involving all stakeholders from the start, thus enhancing (local) capacity building. Strategic alliances between the various stakeholders are needed to jointly encounter the challenges of future tourism.

A new approach to tourism development and management - Integrated Total Quality Tourism Management (ITQT) – has been developed to respond to these challenges. ITQT is a holistic approach to tourism development and management which integrates socio-cultural, environmental and economic aspects in a more comprehensive way than currently generally recognized. It involves a genuine bottom-up approach and aims to generate the 3-tier benefit SEE (Socio-culturally enriching, Environmentally sustainable, Economically viable).

The concept of ITQT proposes a sustainable approach to tourism, generating multiple benefits. However, tourism is not necessarily desirable or feasible for every place. Therefore, each community should examine according to the aspects outlined by the World Tourism Organization (1993) if the project in question is feasible, sustainable and desirable with regard to socio-cultural, environmental and economic aspects.

From the full range of powerful management tools available, just a few have been selected here by way of example: Environmental Impact Assessment (EIA), Carrying Capacity Analysis (CCA), Life-Cycle Analysis (LCA), Environmental Audits (EA)). However, this does not imply that the tools indicated here are considered the most efficient *per se*. The decision made as to the tools to be selected should take the specific context into account and decide what is most appropriate for it.

Tourism as a 3-fold benefit generator

A genuinely sustainable approach needs to be socio-culturally enriching, environmentally sustainable and economically viable.

— *Socio-culturally enriching*: To be sustainable, development needs to include the people who implement, manage and control it. It would be difficult, even impossible, to establish a workable model of a sustainable business community if individual commitment to the spirit of sustainable development is not ensured through understanding of its goals. Maximizing the awareness and involvement of all concerned, thus encouraging a new ethic, must therefore be a prerequisite for action. A community should not only share a common geography, but the same values and expectations.

— *Environmentally sustainable*: To be sustainable, development needs to include the natural environment, on which it depends. Renewable and non-renewable resources must be managed with sensitivity and common sense and in a way that takes a very long-term view. A new classification of priorities is required, i.e. one that does not always place the environment second, but makes it an important element of day-to-day business. The real and wider damage of ecological disruption must be quantified and internalized in the cost of consumer goods.

— *Economically viable*: To be sustainable, development must include a commitment to promoting economic prosperity. This is essential if the funds needed to protect the natural environment and to sustain the population living in are to be generated.

Integrated long-term planning, management and monitoring

An anticipatory, preventive and visionary approach is needed to planning, management and monitoring. When discussing importance of maintaining a high-quality environment in sustaining tourism activity it is appropriate to consider 'thresholds' or 'critical loads' of tourism activity.

A given environmental impact (or combination of impacts) can be tolerated up to a point beyond which the environmental resource suffers and ceases to be a positive attraction and the tourism activity that relies on it has to substitute other resources or decline.

Various critical loads or 'carrying capacities' should be considered such as:

— The 'physical carrying capacity', i.e. the absolute limit on tourist numbers that a resource can cope with.

— The 'ecological carrying capacity', i.e. the level of visits beyond which unacceptable ecological impacts will occur, either as a result of the tourists themselves or the amenities they require.

— The 'host social carrying capacity', i.e. the level beyond which unacceptable change will start affecting the social ways of life of the residents.

— The 'tourist social carrying capacity', i.e. the level beyond which visitor satisfaction drops unacceptably as a result of overcrowding.

It is equally important to monitor tourism's adverse impact continuously, by quantifying and internalizing the costs, in order to obtain a realistic picture of the situation and a solid basis for future plans. As an answer to the possible extinction of 40% of known species in the next 50 years and the recognition of the close link to tourism, the 4th conference of the parties of the biodiversity convention took Travel & Tourism into account for the first time. 170 countries agreed on establishing a common framework and guidelines for sustainable tourism. A protocol is planned for the next conference in 2000, including an eco-balance aiming at quantifying the damage caused by tourism.

Stakeholder Theory

The Stakeholder approach attempts to include everybody with a stake in the issue so that all their needs are considered when setting objectives and everybody is engaged in finding and implementing solutions. A dialogue should be developed to ensure that all parties are involved and contribute. Resources should no longer be considered goods for which no one has specific responsibility. If it is recognized that the environment is being degraded everybody should feel responsible for taking the first step to protect it. Strategic alliances and networking are needed to jointly take care of fragile areas of great value.

This can be achieved with the help of:

— 'Socialization', meaning that each member of the community not only welcomes and accepts the measures taken, but also contributes and helps to implement them.

— 'Actorization', meaning that relations with interest groups and the exchange of opinions are established and harmonized in order to mobilize these groups for joint ventures and long-term plans to establish efficient networking.

— 'Dialogue-ization', meaning that the dialogue between industry, government and science is stimulated in order to minimize multi-interpretations of facts and to encourage information exchange, advanced research and creation of a platform for dialogue.

In view of the rapid growth of tourism and the concomitant opportunities and dangers, together with factors such as an ever increasing number of stakeholders and the depletion of natural resources and extinction of species, there is an urgent need for integrated and preventive approaches as well as for strategic alliances and networking among the various stakeholders in order for joint responsibility to be established for fragile areas of special value, whilst at the same time creating income and job opportunities.

Integrated Total Quality Tourism Management has been proposed as a holistic approach to tourism development and management. Building on methodologies such as the stakeholder theory, it aims to preserve the environment whilst allowing sustainable socio-economic development. The challenge is to use strategic alliances in a preventive way rather than as end-of-pipe solution to avoid disastrous and irreversible effects implying immense costs and losses.

Planning Framework for Regulating Environmental Effects : The Case of Canary Islands

A traditional temptation when regulating the tourist industry and its environmental effects consists of resorting to regional planning instruments as the only framework for consensus. Whilst recognising that island regional planning is now a necessity and an instrument that can prevent major dysfunctions in the rational use of resources, what does not seem recommendable is for this to become the only framework for discussion among the different actors that make up an activity as complex as the tourist industry.

Constraining the debate on tourist development in the islands to a matter of town planning or resource planning, presupposes that an initial analysis has been established in which the initial hypotheses will always concern aspects related to part of the tourist industry, infrastructures and accommodation, neglecting many other factors that enable us to define the product or the different products that make up the final image of the island destination. This simplistic view feeds off the tremendous social and economic tensions that are created in new destinations.

The financial, administrative and jurisdictional scale and complexity of these processes has meant that most island destinations have been mere observers of operations that were beyond their control. And this is exactly what has happened in the Canary Islands. In the seventies, the Canary Islands started building areas suitable for mass tourism, with the firm support of the public sector focussed basically on creating transport infrastructure and the appropriate conditions by adopting the corresponding planning. Around 1986, the islands had nearly two hundred planning initiatives that covered an area of fifty five thousand hectares (55,000 Ha), reaching a potential capacity of nearly four million accommodation units. This kind of planning madness was typical of an age that has left a profound mark on how to organise tourism. At that time, the process started to take a down-turn and the figures for potential capacity started to undergo a substantial reduction, although they were still way above the real possibilities, not only of the land and resources, but also above the possibilities of social and economic stability.

One only has to recall that the amount of land currently developed for tourist purposes is around twelve thousand hectares and accommodation in the Canary Islands is around three-hundred and fifty thousand beds. In conditions such as these, planning has become a perverse instrument, in that it qualifies an excessive growth of total accommodation units that is beyond all control, and which are only subject to "market forces". In these conditions, competition for space emerges as a key factor in tourism planning, which made the Canary Island Natural Spaces Act and the Island Zoning Plans Act necessary in 1992. This legislation led to the creation of the Canary Island Network of Protected Natural Spaces, made up of 145 Areas and accounting for 40.4% of the total surface area of the Islands altogether.

In terms of results, the main positive effect is obtained by the Natural Spaces Act, which managed to remove a large proportion of expectant land from the disproportionate discourse of tourist development. Dialogue with the rest of the region, however, uses the Regional Zoning Plans as a vehicle. With the exception of the case of Lanzarote, which managed to adopt its Plan in 1994, the tensions generated by the growth of tourism were obvious in all the other Plans, provoking endless processes of adaptation and disproportionate administrative red-tape, which in some cases has lasted more than a decade. The burocratisation of regional planning instruments and processes is clearly due to the expectations generated for tourist developments, which have once again reached new highs in recent years.

To get a true idea of the enormous accommodation infrastructure boom, one only has to consider the fact that, in the next few years, the Islands will account for nearly three quarters of all tourist investment on the Spanish coastline.Current estimates are 283,000 million pesetas ($) for building new hotels on the Canary Island coast, of which 108,000 is for Tenerife, 56,000 for Gran Canaria, 40,000 for Fuerteventura and 11,000 for Lanzarote. The next Spanish regions in the ranking are a long way behind the total numbers for the Canary Islands as a whole, such as the coast of Granada (20,000) or Alicante (14,000).

A more detailed analysis of the situation, in the light of these magnitudes, suggests that we are not really talking about tourism, but rather of property operations characterised by the need to make "safe" investments, attracted by the image of a sector in continuous growth and enhanced by factors that are external to the industry like the special tax regulations in the Islands and the need to convert capital hidden in pesetas before the Euro comes into force as the single currency.

So, new accommodation infrastructure is the driving force of this induced growth in tourism, which clearly suggests that there is an absence of criteria applicable to tourist strategy and that there is no clear model or tourist product that is more suitably adapted to the situation. In fact, most of these new operations contradict the spirit of the Canary Island Tourism Act, which openly opts for adopting environmental criteria, increasing the quality of the supply and rationalising growth in accordance to the specificities of the Islands.

Authorising excessive new tourist beds cannot be justified by market requirements either. In the area of planning, the figures used are for peak occupation, which is between 90% and 95%, when we should really use the average figures, which are only just over 70% for all accommodation categories. These exaggerated expectations of growth, which exceed the phenomenon of mass tourism that occurred in the Islands in the 70's in absolute terms, have radicalised the social debate on future prospects.

Many different initiatives and responses have emerged in response to a phenomenon of this magnitude, including the Lanzarote initiative, whereby they adopted a moratorium on the growth of the accommodation sector, following the example of the process started in the Balearic

Islands. But, even taking into consideration the incalculable demonstrative value of this measure, aimed at establishing a cooling off period, we are really perplexed as we see how the enormous pressure to develop far exceeds the capacity of institutional measures, as one of the first consequences of the moratorium has been to speed up the administrative process for consolidated projects in order not to miss the legal deadlines for the measure, bringing forward the launching of 11,000 new beds onto the market.

This is certainly not the desired outcome, as the island's strategic plan itself, called "Lanzarote in the Biosphere", warned that it was time to curb the process because rapid growth in tourist numbers and the development of new resorts on the coast has led to a 5% increase in developed land in little more than a decade and regional land density has increased more than 60%. And this is despite the fact that the Island Regional Zoning Plan declassified more than 200,000 tourist beds on the Island in 1991.

Another typical reaction in all this confusion is to attack the concept of mass tourisms, offering the alternative of new forms and products based on the concept of eco-tourism or rural tourism. These trends, which of course are very valid in many emerging island destinations, are a supplementary risk in the case of consolidated destinations. With the exception of the case of El Hierro, an island which, right from the beginning, opted for a low density tourist model based on refurbishing their building heritage, giving ones blessing to these new options in a region that receives 11 million tourists a year means adding another penetration factor in sensitive areas, with unpredictable consequences. The problem lies in the fact that, with a model of this kind, a scattered tourist occupation of rural areas and of the few virgin landscapes will lead to a demand for infrastructures that have thus far been considered unnecessary.

But, apart from the new danger arising from a generalisation of rural accommodation, we find that new tourist products are appearing, based on the attraction of the new stereotyped ecological or natural tourism. The risk involved in an uncontrolled promotion of this kind of supply in islands with fragile and limited resources is considerable. But, what could be of even more concern is that this is an induced supply with no scientific base, an intuitive response to a foreseeable deterioration of conventional tourist products.

These opinions are supported by a study carried out for Lanzarote in 1997, sponsored by the island's association of hoteliers in co-operation with the Ministry of Industry, Trade and Tourism, in which Insula participated too. One of the objectives set out was to establish appropriate methodologies for studying, with greater precision the expectations raised by the destination of Lanzarote as a differentiated tourist product, and to identify the main gaps existing between expectations and perception. Environmental aspects were analysed with special attention, as surveys carried out up until that moment had not differentiated this aspect.

Apart from classical aspects of the Canary Islands product, such as the preponderance of the climate and accommodation factors, attention should be paid to the high expectations granted to the landscape and the environmental quality of the destination. But this latter aspect should be defined more precisely, because if we take a closer look, we will see that expectations of the exotic nature of the destination, nature activities and cultural aspects are low. If we go deeper into this perspective, we find that the largest environmental gaps were those concerning accommodation environments, complexes and resorts.

Results like these, applicable with certain nuances to the rest of the Canary Islands, show the distance that separates the tourist planning and marketing carried out by Lanzarote from real expectations of tourists. Opting for enhancing quality with an environment-related supply led to enormous investment being made in the Canary Islands, in tracks, lookout spots and public infrastructures in natural spaces and areas of great scenic value, when what is really needed, and urgently, is an enhanced environmental integration of tourist centres, where factors like aesthetics and integration of complexes, noise, waste, transport and urban refurbishment are the priority demands. In fact, this is the philosophy laid down in several excellency plans that have been initiated in the main tourist cities, and possibly explain the successful acceptance that has been given to the Local Agenda 21 experience in Calvia, a tourist district on the island of Majorca, in the Balearic Islands.

All of this leads us to believe that planning and tools like marketing, which have an enormous influence on designing the tourist supply, should be based on scientific criteria and methodologies that are more in line with the reality of each island. Experience shows us daily that the enormous diversity of island situations makes it necessary to be very cautious with the more perverse aspects arising from planning, or the homogenising temptation based on the importance of models. Island products are clearly highly diverse, and this is precisely what gives them their strength as a whole. This means that the Canary Islands. should not, for example, insist on selling an image of an exotic and idyllic destination, but rather, it should find the elements that really differentiate it from other products. A survey carried out by the Seychelles Tourist Marketing Administration for European travellers supports this idea when it established that the top ten exotic and idyllic destinations were Mauritius, Hawaii, Maldives, Cuba, Guadeloupe, Martinique, Bali, Sri Lanka, Seychelles and Tahiti.

The key words in new strategies for improving destinations like the Canary Islands are not their exotic nature, eco-tourism or nature-related products. In their stead, advances must be made in terms of refurbishment, regeneration, quality enhancement and diversification, a new framework that must cease to use the failure of the current system of conventional planning as its foundation.

Infrastructures

In the planning framework, an increasing importance is given to infrastructure-related decisions, their conception and design. Tourist destination managers are gradually realising that a strict land, protectionist of the environment and built heritage, is of little use if the size of tourist resorts, inland and maritime transport systems, accesses and water and energy infrastructures, go beyond the possibilities of the territory and degrade the tourist product. To large infrastructure decisions, we must add the design factor, as we can frequently find solutions which are aesthetically and conceptually inappropriate for the local reality. Mostly they are imported and camouflaged solutions that take island harmony apart and irretrievably mortgage their future.

The continuing neglect of the predominant role that infrastructure plays in designing a tourism model becomes evident in the strange relations that many peripheral islands have with their mainland states. If, for instance, we analyse the destination of the European Union's Structural Funds for islands, we see investments, under the pretext of improving the tourist sector, are usually assigned to grandiose works of infrastructure (roads, air transport, electricity grid, etc.), whose adaptation to the island situation is doubtful, which are difficult to maintain and which involve extraordinary regional impact.

The conviction that the development of infrastructures is a constant in the island development equation is proving a fallacy that entails serious problems. These errors of simplification have already been shown from the experiences derived from the Remote Island Development Act (RIDA) in Japan, and the Canary Islands are currently undergoing a similar process. Airport infrastructure and road transport planning are two good examples of this.

In the heat of the island debate about the urgent need to limit the growth of tourist constructions and land use, in Tenerife, plans are afoot to extend the new airports to triple their current capacity. The new airport master plans lays down the number of passenger movements at around 25 million, which destroys any attempt at regulation.

The peculiar view of the islander, who is used to shortages, and a deregulated supply of external aid, together, forms an explosive cocktail for extremely fragile and vulnerable areas. An extreme example of this can be seen in the island of La Gomera, where an airport has been built for tourist purposes, but which is not operational due to lack of demand, because sea communications have been improved extremely quickly. The local authorities have even proposed public subsidies for airlines.

The useless environmental, economic and social impact of the project was hotly expressed in the process of drafting the Ecoplan, a useless task at a time when the local authorities thought that they could not waste Community aid so shortly after joining the European Union. These are very common mistakes to be found in all islands, all over the world. These risks are as common as those involved in internal transport models.

Inland transport is probably one of the major environmental risk factors for island tourist destinations. Importing of unadapted mobility systems and oversizing of infrastructures induced by tourist activity always has devastating effects in such fragile and limited territories. According to the Spanish Traffic Directorate-general Yearbook, Balearic islands head the national ranking with a rate of 916 vehicles per 1000 inhabitants, followed by the two Canary Islands provinces with 650 in Las Palmas and 688 in Tenerife. But when we analyse the density of vehicles, we find that the Canary Islands also go to extreme figures, reaching up to 205.4 vehicles per km^2, that is twice the Spanish average, that is 128, and four times the European average, that is 51.5 vehicles per km^2.

Road density follows the same trend. Canary Islands' road network consists of 4,362 km of roads, with an average of 0.58 km/km^2, a very high ratio if we think that 42% of the territory is protected, and therefore road density in these areas is obviously lower. Nevertheless, we must clarify that this is common feature of tourist islands, where road densities are always extremely high, like on Martinica (1.4 km/km^2), and on Madeira (1.7 km/km^2).

Effects induced by tourist activity are particularly clear in the case of Lanzarote. Within the "Lanzarote in the Biosphere" plan, it is possible to notice the "over-motorisation" of the island and the lack of island mobility planning criteria. There are 800 vehicles per 1000 inhabitants, going beyond the average of most European countries; global traffic reaches 685 million vehicles/km per year, a disproportionate number for a territory so vulnerable to mobility-induced impacts; tourists cover an average of

49 km daily doubling the available figures relative to other Mediterranean tourist destinations; the number of cars increased of 65% between 1988 and 1996; public transport can only manage 26% of displacements. Estimations show that tourist rented cars are alone 40% of the total motor vehicle traffic on the island, although they are just 20% of the total number of cars.

In spite of this circumstances, are being built and planned 227 km of new roads financed in agreement with the Spanish Government and with a high -financing percentage from the Community funds, which in theory are intended to help the less favoured islands and must finance actions with a high content of environmental infrastructures.

Nevertheless, we must take into account that, on tourist islands, many other factors contribute to transport characterisation apart from the above mentioned ones. Route design and use of traditional access systems, which on the other hand can be an important tourist resource, decisively contribute to the safeguard of basic landscape assets in each destination.

Let's take the example of Minorca, where there is an equally high road density, 0.53 km/km2, 21% higher than the Balearic Islands' average, which is mainly due to the high dispersion of the 39 main tourist settlements, with a total of 360 km of finished roads.

In spite of this high density, the road network is excellently integrated. The tourist development strategy laid down was particularly concerned about the route and access system, and the original two-century-old routes have been practically left unchanged. Within the framework of this plan, a poll was taken among tourists. The result of this poll pointed out that tourists have different mobility criteria, and they value more positively low speeds and landscape's environmental elements.

Conscious of the need to give long-term answers to the island mobility problems, Insula launched a project called TATE-Islands (Tourism and Transport Equilibrium in Island Regions), centred on the small Italian islands, Madeira, Crete, Balearic Islands and Canary Islands. These territories have been explicitly selected as they are areas of application for large-scale demonstration projects on renewable energies and alternative transports within the White Paper for a Community Strategy and Action Plan, subtitled "Energy for the Future: Renewable Sources of Energy". The objectives outlined within this project are: to define the possible sustainable mobility scenarios for tourist islands (SMT), to support innovation in the field of alternative collective vehicles (zero and low emission vehicles – both electric and hybrid), to establish the means to support no-traffic solutions (pedestrian and bicycles) to develop large-scale demonstration projects. Priority areas of action are centred on the accessibility of sensitive and protected areas, historic centres and big tourist resorts.

It must be admitted that the relative abundance of resources assigned to conventional infrastructures is in sharp contrast with the generalised delay in implementing information technologies (IT). We do know, however, that islands are irremediably called upon to play a leading role in this new revolution. For example, one only has to emphasise the fact that in the process carried out by the Small and Remote Islands of Japan, information technologies have become a basic factor in the new tourist strategy, with collateral influences in the diversification and promotion of cultural, and even agro-industrial, products (healthy foods, medicinal plants, tropical fruits, flowers...).

It is a fact that introducing islands into the Information Society is one of the major challenges of the next few years. New information technologies make it possible to break down the barriers of general and specialised information that, in the past, have accentuated the isolation of islands. The cost of new information technologies is now affordable for small communities and isolated users. And this is a great advantage for islands, because the new economy of the global market will be based more on the supply and exchange of immaterial, knowledge related goods. In the near future, a large part of marketing and trade will be done electronically, allowing easy access to the global market for island communities through telematic networks.

In the case of the Canary Islands, there is already one example in an advanced stage of development. The Tenerife Cabildo (Island Government), aware of the need to respond to new trends and, at the same time, create scenarios in which tourist activity can act as a vector to enhance the value of rural products and in creating landscape, in 1998, designed the Tenerife Rural Plan – Quality Network. The Plan identifies 40 rural enclaves that can be visited, but which, at the same time, are connected with and open to the outside, thanks to a powerful telematic network that even includes e-commerce services.

The idea is to recover the landscape and the singularities of the rural environment as a tourist asset, but without degrading the space. Building visitable, or network connected centres includes such diverse aspects as the wine centre, the potato centre, the honey centre, the biodiversity centre, water galleries, wheat mills, music handicrafts, tobacco, fishing, fish-farming, etc. But, in the context of the Information Society, the strategy of enhancing the quality and diversifying tourism in islands is not an isolated occurrence. With this new vision, island tourist destinations can help each other to become stronger; their extreme diversity becomes an outstanding instrument in the global market. There are important infrastructure barriers however, that must be overcome to convert this potential into a tangible reality. That is why Insula, under the slogan "Share to compete", is promoting the MEDIS Project co-financed by the European Commission. The basic objectives of this initiative is to cover the strategy outlined above. They focus on:

— Providing an advanced picture of the state of the art about telecommunications and telematic infrastructures and services in European islands.

— Facilitating the provision of community services and the use of telematics in different sectors and activities such as Tourism, health, transport and business. Related to commercial and tourist systems and business, participation of local authorities and public bodies

— Comparing the results with the figures provided at national level by the European Survey of the Information Society.

— Profiling alternative network telecom infrastructure and services in the European islands with potential for use in IS applications.

Tourism and protected spaces

Despite its small size, the Canary Island chain houses a natural heritage of extraordinary value. Its outstanding ecosystems and the flora and fauna, including unique species, has generated a strong spirit of regional conservation among the Canary Island and international communities. In fact, the Canary Islands have one of the greatest biodiversities of the Earth's temperate regions in relation to the small surface area they cover. It is also considered a first class biodiversity centre due to the large number of endemic species to be found there. By way of reference, of the 11,600 land species known in the Archipelago (without counting protistas and monerons), approximately 3,700 are endemic to the Islands. All together, the catalogues include 433 endangered taxa of Canary Island flora (381 vegetable species and 52 fungi and lichens) and 566 species of fauna (430 invertebrates and 136 vertebrates), for which conservation measures will be taken, based on the degree of the threat.

Recognition of these values is reflected in the enormous effort that has been made in the area of conservation and management of natural resources. A framework has been created of different instruments of protection, such as the Canary Island Network of Protected Natural Spaces, the "Natura 2000" Network and Biosphere Reserves. Although all these measure have the same objective, there are small differences between them in both the strategies they use and their scope of action. The Canary Island Network of Protected Natural Spaces is aimed at developing an integral management model, with the emphasis on public use and tourism. It attempts to make the conservation of Canary Island biodiversity compatible with the protection of cultural and aesthetic values and with supplying society with environmental material goods and services.

The main priority of the Natura 2000 Network, however, is to preserve European biodiversity, that is, the habitats and species of community interest. Although it also intends to guarantee the conservation of these values through sustainable development, it acts in a more selective fashion on the habitats and species of the Canary Islands. Fundamentally, it focuses on endangered habitats

The Biosphere Reserves represent a different case. The declaration of the island of Lanzarote, along with the island of Minorca in the Balearic Islands, was proposed in 1995, in order to help create a model of harmonious development of regional tourism, which is why the reserve encompasses the whole island, including tourist resorts and populations. In the case of the island of El Hierro, on the other hand, the first island to be declared a reserve in the new millennium, the objective was to consolidate an integral model in which the emphasis is on rural production of high value added, where tourism is incorporated in the economy as a complementary factor.

Technological innovation and conservation stand side by side in El Hierro in a surprising manner. One only has to point out that this is the first island in Europe where a project is being developed aimed at covering all the island's energy consumption needs with energy from renewable sources, or the El Hierro 100% digital plan, which includes a network of nature conservation centres, or the ambitious El Hierro Zero Waste programme.

The work carried out by the Canary Island Government's Department of the Environment indicates that there are several factors that are directly derived from tourism, that represent an important risk for the Canary Island environment In such delicate island areas, introduced species affect the natural dynamic of ecosystems, producing serious consequences, such as the extinction of populations or species and the degradation of the soil. Another example of environmental impact comes from man-made hybridisation, which now occurs more clearly with Canary Island flora because of the fact that it is inappropriately used for ornamental purposes. But, apart from these more evident factors, it is the public and tourist use of these spaces that is the real challenge for managing an area that receives 11 million tourists a year. The Teide National Park, in the island of Tenerife, is a clear example of this: it received over 2.2 million visitors in 1998, which is a real challenge for management. As you can see, this is a completely different problem from those faced by other islands and emerging destinations, where eco-tourism products are generated for much smaller numbers of tourists. In this case, there are two possibilities: implement strict deterrent policies governing access (now necessary in many places), or find new formulae capable of combining conservation with the maintenance of an acceptable tourist experience.

A magnificent example of integrating tourist infrastructures in sensitive areas is the Lanzarote Network of Tourist Centres. In the seventies, a network of visitors' centres was designed in the island, which are characterised by the fact that they are so well integrated in the environment and by the fact that they were based on implanting formal patterns of the local culture. As Cesar Manrique, artistic genius and author of these works, said: "I am like the hand that expresses the geology and the feeling of the island". It is surprising that some of these works, which are now emblematic for the island, were done on sites such as a former landfill located in a volcanic pipe, or an old, disused quarry. The strangest fact is that these centres now receive an enormous flow of visitors, over a million tourists a year in some cases. But their clever design has allowed people to be concentrated in each space, avoiding the dispersion of visitors, with the added advantage that they provide a high quality tourist experience. In this case, Lanzarote has been imaginative, it has taken advantage of the possibility of recovering apparently degraded spaces through tourism, rather than give way to the systematic and compulsive temptation to colonise and occupy virgin areas.

Another example of new generation projects aimed at resolving the paradigm of public and tourist use of natural spaces is to be found in the island of Tenerife. A visitors' centre is presently being designed in Punta de Teno that brings together the criteria used in Lanzarote with telematics and the latest technologies in the areas of sustainable construction and transport. The centre aims to concentrate the tourist activity of a small area that receives half a million tourists a year by land and a more extensive marine area where the tourist activity of whale watching attracts 2.3 million tourists a year, making it the most heavily used enclave in the world.

In this context, a centre has been designed that has been dug into the depths of the Punta de Teno volcano, called "Window on the Sea". The architecture has been defined as silent, as it has no external elements, all transport is electric and powerful telematic means give three dimensional access in real time to the entire marine and terrestrial environment. The Window on the Sea, in turn, will be connected with eight other windows, on other islands of the world, also in real time. It is therefore, an example of integrating information technology into new resources to favour a balanced design of tourism in very fragile surroundings.

El Hierro too, provides us with ingenious solutions of harmony between tourism and traditional activities. On this island, declared a biosphere reserve, there is marine fish reserve (Mar de las Calmas) that has been promoted by the guild of fishermen. To guarantee adequate use of the space, the fishermen themselves have become the tourist managers of the area, creating a surprising model of tourism and artesenal fishing. This model has also been successfully developed in the Medas Islands, on the east coast of Spain.

The island of Tenerife has also developed a global model, as the shoreline and the marine environment of the island are usually neglected by protection and harmony measures designed for terrestrial environments. In 1996, the Tenerife Cabildo (Island Government) launched a programme called Tenerife and the Sea , aimed at establishing a broad consensus among all actors that operate on the shoreline: the tourist sector, fishing, traditional activities, sports, transport, etc. The development of the programme was based on demonstration projects to establish references for public and private initiatives.

In the area of tourism, these include projects like soft accesses to the sea, protecting the sea bed, a network of visitable sites, fisheries reserves, recovering traditional bathing systems and demolishing swimming pools built on the shoreline, effluent control, recovery of historic building heritage and the development of an advanced information system with various telematic resources.

Trinomial energy-water-tourism

In the last years, the trinomial energy-water-tourism has been representing a great challenge for tourist islands. This new specialisation, added to population growth, places islands in an extremely vulnerable position. Energy and water, because of their territorial, environmental and economic implications, have always represented a central element of the insular dilemma. The problem of freshwater supply affects small islands more than big ones, as they have a large part of the water-related problems. According to the works developed within the UNESCO's International Hydrological Programme, these difficulties are specially expressed by islands smaller than 1,000 km^2 and narrower than 20 km. Local hydrological values are also very different from one island to another. In the Mediterranean area, for instance, the most frequent values are between 400 and 600 mm. But the worst thing is that the largest differences can appear in successive years or on two different sides of the island or even at different altitudes.

To overcome these difficulties the small islands have developed a very complex culture of water to take maximum advantage from their scarce resources: tanks, rainwater reservoirs, impluvia, etc.. Furthermore, we know the need to use solutions as the water transportation in tank ships employed from long time to bring water to small Italian and Greek islands, or submarine water conducts bringing water from the continent to the islands of Elba, Tabarca or to some Dalmatian islands for example. Recent tourist developments, like those of Djerba, lead to mobilisation of water resources from the mainland to guarantee the needed supply.

Malta, for example, has an area of 246 km^2 and a population density higher than 1,200 people/km^2 outside the tourist area. The island is in reality a great calcareous slab, fissured and therefore with little capacity to retain water. Or Lanzarote, an Atlantic island with an area of 900 km2 where water supply for its more than 45,000 tourist accommodations and 90,000 inhabitants comes almost exclusively from desalination. These are extreme cases but they clearly show the current trend of a large part of the Mediterranean and European islands, and exemplify possible risks and dependences of the future.

Nevertheless, water deficit due to growing tourism on islands, generates new risks. It is evident that new demands in island economies introduce a factor of competition with the traditional agricultural activities. It is also serious that vital water supplies are diverted from fragile ecosystems and high-value wetlands, and we know well the risks derived from water extractions in the coast.

The Canary Islands are not an exception. Water shortage due to canalising and channelling is a point that deserves special attention. Intense manipulation and extraction of this natural resource, accelerated by tourism, turned it into a factor of destruction and alteration of the environment seriously affecting wildlife. It is not difficult to see the effects on wild flora. Willow woods were once growing in the bottom of most valleys, from the high areas to their lower limit marked by the succulent vegetation area (cardonales and tabaibales), and at present they are confined only in a few places and their distribution is discontinuous from the medium-altitude to the higher areas. Now, after water canalisation, the places were the original willows were once thriving, are invaded by brambles and reed beds. Fauna has also been harmed by water shortage. Several invertebrates directly depend on water, especially those living in valley beds. Water shortage can harm several hundred species, many of which are Canary Islands' endemics. Birds also suffer the effects of drought, many of them having a great interest for being exclusive of the islands or of the Macaronesian Region. Situations similar to those of the Canary Islands are frequent and have similar effects. Islands like Corfu, Minorca, Elba or Rhodes, have also tourist densities higher than 100 beds per km^2.

To these new needs of the tourist demand, problems caused by seasonality must be added. In Majorca water consumption is estimated in 90,000 cubic metres in winter and rise to 130.000 in the tourist season. But the influence of tourism is not only limited to a greater number of consumers: it also affects the type of consumption. Normal islanders' standards (100-125 litres) are multiplied after the arrival of tourism, and often exceed 250 litres. Furthermore, we must take into account that tourism demands an endless supply and, because of the leisure facilities such as swimming pools, golf courses and greens, even when there is enough water, there are high losses in main supply.

These subjects have been a basic concern of the twenty-second United Nations General Assembly, within the special session exclusively dedicated to islands, whose objective was the re-examination of the Barbados Action Plan.

A great portion of the world's islands declared that aspects related to tourism, water and energy management would clearly determine island future sustainable development. The report of the Global Conference on the Sustainable Development of Small Island Developing States, revised during that special session, establishes two pressing objectives:

— Encourage the development and acquisition of appropriate technology and training for cost-effective desalination and rainwater collection to provide sufficiently high quality potable freshwater, including opportunities for technology interchange among Small Island Developing States.

— Improve access to environmentally sound and energy efficient technologies for the production and delivery of freshwater.

These aspects related to water management demand pressing attention and perfectly fit into the new view of islands' energy perspective. The Island Solar Summit took place on the island of Tenerife, jointly organised by ITER,

INSULA, the Tenerife Island Government, the UNESCO and the World Solar Programme. It approached for the first time the energy-water issue on islands jointly, and its relationship with tourist activity. For island people, it's now evident the need to give a reasonable answer to two problems posed at the some time. From now on, we must speak of water and energy on the same plane.

From the energy point of view, we know that islands are characterised by:

— Isolation and dependence
— Limited range of energy resources
— Specialisation of economies
— Limited markets
— Highly sensitive environment
— Inefficient use of energy resources

These characteristics dangerously burden islands' opening to tourism. In energy terms, risks for the economies and the environment are too high when we resort to artificial water. Tourism influence on energy consumption in small and medium-sized islands is surely high. In Lanzarote, for instance, it was possible to achieve a differentiated characterisation of energy consumption: 7.7 kwh/day per local inhabitant and 11.5 kwh/day per tourist. The case of St. Lucia island is truly enlightening in this regard. In St. Lucia, hotels account for 35% of the island's total energy consumption, and 80% of this consumption is accounted for by air conditioning.

However, islands' peculiarities can help resolving such a difficult problem. Among islands' advantages there are:

— Abundant renewable energy sources

— Modularity and adaptability to the island scale of the solutions and technologies based on renewable energies.

— Island economies don't have any sector with high energy demand.

— If we consider islands as a whole, their water-renewables combined market is possibly the largest in the world.

Within this context, mentioned insularity features are in favour of an advisable alliance between renewable energies and water production through desalination. An alliance that is still more necessary in the increasing tourist specialisation framework of many islands. There are many economic and technological reasons supporting this idea. Typical data per cubic meter of fresh water are 8-15 kWh for commercial distillation (heat consuming processes) and 4-7 kWh for commercial membrane systems (electricity consuming processes). These numbers show the large amount of supplementary energy needed by certain islands in order to secure themselves a sufficient water supply. But we also know that wind energy is a high competitive form of producing energy, even in islands with a low average wind speed. The usage of wind turbines to power medium sized desalination plants is perfect, and several pilot plants are being developed, as well as hybrid systems using PV panels and wind generators to produce fresh water.

We should also take into account that water storage, compared to electricity or heat, has the added advantage of being quite a simple matter. Desalinated water storage is a simple issue for most islands, and is an excellent solution to technologically harmonize the use of renewable energy sources on a large scale and guarantee freshwater supply under small islands' variable consumption conditions. We already know that renewable energy sources suffer from irregular energy supply. But with an increasing demand for water, the penetration of renewable energies can be supported. Water production plants may play a major role as variable loads for any system, helping to absorb production peaks. As water can be stored without difficulties for longer periods, water demand peaks do not affect water production rates.

To strengthen this alliance and develop adequate market niches in island tourist destinations, in the framework of the European Commission's Altener and Energy programmes, two innovative initiatives, co-ordinated by Insula, have been formalised. The Island 2010 project, aimed at promoting 100% renewable tourist destination initiatives, and the OPET European Island network, aimed at establishing adequate frameworks of consensus between the tourist industry, local authorities, services suppliers, technological institutes and local consultants. Preferential areas of action for the next four years are: desalination with renewable energy in hotel establishments, alternative transport, renewable energy applications in protected spaces, energy efficiency and renewable energy in the hotel sector.

As an example of the tourist industry's capacity to adopt new behaviour patterns in islands, based on the criteria of sustainable development, it is essential to underline the experience of the Institute of Responsible Tourism. The IRT was created with the support of UNESCO after the World Conference on Sustainable Tourism, held in Lanzarote in 1995. One of the most interesting achievements of the IRT has been to develop the Responsible Tourism System for application in hotels. The system is based on a set of standards, with requirements that are fully in line with ISO 14000 or EMAS standards, which make enormous advances in the commitment of the hotel industry to their destinations.

The requisites to be applied cover aspects like:

— Water saving and quality
— Energy efficiency policy
— Renewable energy sources
— Minimising and recycling waste
— Emission and effluent control
— Reduction of environmental impacts
— Noise and disturbance limitation
— Integrating establishments in the landscape
— Integrating supply in the local culture
— Good purchasing policy
— Compatible and responsible tourist services
— Sustainable telematic applications .

6

Sustainable Tourism Development in Small Islands

The Programme of Action for the Sustainable Development of Small Island Developing States, in chapter VIII, acknowledges the important contribution of tourism to the development of many small island developing States, while noting that "if not properly planned and managed, tourism could significantly degrade the environment on which it is so dependent". In this vein, it espouses actions to be promoted at the national, regional and international levels in order to ensure the viability of the sector and its harmonious development with the cultural and natural endowments of small island developing States.

Progress Achieved

Economic Development

Tourism is often identified as a promising growth sector in small island developing States. It offers one of the few opportunities for economic diversification in very small islands. Tourism has many linkages with other economic sectors, and if integrated into national development plans with adequate provisions for intersectoral linkages, it can contribute to the growth of all tourism-related activities in all of the major economic sectors - agriculture, including fishing, industry and services, including transportation. At present, the extent of tourism activities in small island developing States varies widely between geographical regions as well as between countries within regions. Likewise, the economic benefits derived from tourism are diverse. In some small island developing States, tourism has become the major contributor to the gross domestic product (GDP), while in others it is still relatively undeveloped.

It is well known that in small island developing States, the scope for economic diversification and growth is limited. Their key constraints are small land areas and small populations. The relatively larger ones have the human resources potential to support a number of economic sectors viably and thus to benefit from linkages of those sectors with the tourism sector. The smaller ones, however, do not have such potential and will therefore have to be more reliant on imports to meet the material demands of the tourism sector. Other things remaining equal, the net benefits, i.e., domestic value-added per visitor, derived by the smaller islands from tourism will be relatively smaller.

The main objectives of the promotion of tourism as a growth sector are to accelerate the growth of national incomes, gainful employment, foreign exchange earnings and government tax revenues. A thorough evaluation of the contribution of tourism in small island developing States with respect to these parameters is at present hampered by the incompleteness of data. In a sample of 29 small island developing States for which data are available, gross direct receipts from tourism as a percentage of GDP ranged from a meagre 1 per cent to 88 percent on the average during the period 1989-1993. In this sample of countries, tourism and tourism-related activities have become the mainstay of the economy in Antigua and Barbuda, Aruba, Barbados, Saint Lucia, the Bahamas, Saint Kitts and Nevis and Seychelles, or mostly in the small island developing States in the Caribbean. Important exceptions apart, tourism makes the least contribution to national income in most of the African and Pacific small island developing States.

With a few exceptions, most small island developing States have realized a fast, although diverse, pace of growth of gross tourism receipts in nominal terms in recent years. During the period 1989-1993, in 24 out of 34 for which data are available, the growth of gross receipts from tourism ranged from 2 per cent to 61 per cent per annum on the average . In most, it exceeded 10 per cent and in 9 it was 15 per cent or more. Generally, but not universally, the fast pace of growth reflects low initial levels of receipts from tourism. Even among those with low initial levels, several countries did not do so well.

In view of the constraints faced by small island developing States in promoting exports of goods in an increasingly competitive and fast-changing international economy, by and large, these States are giving increasing importance to tourism as a source of raising their foreign exchange earnings. The available data show that during the period 1980-1992, for a sample of 26 small island developing States, the percentage increase in the ratio of foreign exchange earnings from tourism to total export earnings ranged from 2 per cent to 453 per cent. In 10 of them, it exceeded 50 per cent. In 1992, the contribution of tourism to total export earnings in 23 countries ranged from a meagre 2 per cent to 83 per cent; in 13 of them it exceeded 25 per cent.

The data on average daily expenditures per visitor for 10 countries ranged from US$ 41 to $304 in 1992. In 1989, average daily expenditures per visitor for 23 small island developing States ranged from $37 to $226. The diversity of performance even in these small samples is significant. It suggests that those countries that want to promote tourism as a growth sector need, in addition to adequate investments in tourism infrastructure, to make greater efforts to enhance the diversity and quality of goods and services they sell to visitors.

Countries that have relatively full employment are less interested in the employment potential of expansion of tourism than those that have substantial unemployment. The employment advantages of tourism are twofold: first, the industry is labour-intensive, and secondly, much of the employment is relatively unskilled. Consequently, investment in tourism produces a higher and faster increase in employment than equal investment in other activities. Tourism creates employment directly in the tourism industry as well as in industries providing goods and services to the tourism industry.

Data on direct employment in the tourism industry is extremely scanty. It may be inferred, however, that the impact of tourism on employment in small island developing States, where tourism makes an important contribution to national income, is considerable. In 15 Caribbean tourist destinations, a total of 77,319 hotel rooms accounted for 88,697 jobs, equivalent to 1.15 jobs per room. With the recent decline in the agriculture sector, in particular sugar and bananas, the relative share of tourism in employment has risen. In the South Pacific, tourism generated 27,500 jobs in direct employment in 1991 in the 10 member countries of the Tourism Council of the South

Pacific (TCSP), with a population of about 5 million. Fiji accounted for 10,340 of this amount.

In the Mediterranean region, overall employment in Cyprus exhibited an upward trend during the period 1980-1992, with the fastest growth occurring in tourism and related services. Employment in these occupations doubled from 33,000 jobs in 1980 to 64,000 in 1992. Hotels, restaurants and retail trade increased their share of employment from 17.9 per cent in 1980 to 24.3 per cent in 1992.

In 1993, the total contribution of tourism to employment in Malta was roughly estimated at about 17 per cent of the labour force. In the African region, the available data for Mauritius and Seychelles indicate that during the period 1990-1994, the share of direct employment in tourism in total employment rose from 3.4 per cent to 4.8 per cent in Mauritius and remained stable at about 18 per cent in Seychelles.

While the employment objective remains important for several small island developing States, the level of wages in the tourism industry is also important. The available information indicates that most jobs created in tourism are low-paying. This is to be expected in countries with high rates of unemployment, particularly of unskilled labour.

The creation of low-paying jobs in the tourism sector in countries with relatively high rates of employment is the result of the strong pull factor of the relatively less physically demanding jobs in the tourism sector from more arduous jobs in the primary sector. This process exerts pressure on producers in the primary sector to modernize and increase capital intensity so as to permit a rising level of real wages; otherwise, the sector will lose its labour force and dwindle. This could marginalize important productive activities such as agriculture and fishing, and weaken the linkages of other sectors with tourism reducing the benefits derived from the tourism industry.

Tourism is likely to play an even more important role in the growth and development of small island developing States if appropriate measures are taken to invigorate other sectors, in particular agriculture and fishing, so that they can more adequately meet tourist demand for consumer goods from domestic sources. Except for the very small ones, small island developing States can, with careful planning and provision of adequate facilities such as credit for mechanization, modernization and diversification, where necessary, support viable agricultural and fishing activities, as well as light manufacturing in addition to tourism. As intersectoral competition raises wage rates and incomes and reduces labour supply to the tourism sector, emphasis can be shifted to up-market tourism, with reliance on a slower rate of growth but of higher-spending visitors.

In evaluating the direct contribution of tourism to national income, gross levels of incomes or gross foreign exchange earnings are much less significant than net earnings after deductions have been made for all necessary foreign exchange expenditures of the tourism industry. The primary leakages of foreign exchange earnings from direct tourist expenditures arise from:

(a) imports of materials and equipment for construction,

(b) imports of consumer goods, particularly food and drink,

(c) repatriation of profits earned by foreign investors,

(d) overseas promotional expenditures and

(e) amortization of external debt incurred in the development of hotels and resorts.

The impact of these leakages varies greatly from country to country depending on the ability of countries to produce the goods and services necessary to meet the needs of the tourism industry. The estimates available for 17 countries or territories presented below show that the higher leakages pertain to small island economies.

Table 1. Leakage of foreign exchange from gross tourism receipts (Percentage)

No.	State	gross tourism receipts in %
1.	Fiji	56
2.	Cook Islands	50
3.	Saint Lucia	45
4.	Mauritius	43
5.	Aruba	41
6.	Hong Kong	41
7.	Jamaica	40
8.	United States Virgin Islands	36
9.	Seychelles	30
10.	Sri Lanka	27
11.	Antigua and Barbuda	25
12.	Cyprus	25
13.	Kenya	22
14.	Republic of Korea	20
15.	New Zealand	12
16.	Yugoslavia	11
17.	Philippines	11

Direct income from tourism provides only a partial picture of the contribution of tourism to national income. A complete picture would call for the estimation of tourism income multipliers in each small island developing State. Since expenditures of tourists give rise to the generation of additional incomes throughout the economy, the incomes and the associated employment thus induced can be considerable. Aside from the savings propensity of the local population, the size of the tourism income multiplier in a particular small island developing State depends on the extent of leakages of tourist expenditures overseas. The less the leakage of direct tourist expenditures, the higher the tourism income multiplier. Because of the complexities relating to the requisite data, however, the estimation of tourism income multipliers is beyond the scope of the present report.

Regional perspectives

At the regional level, the development of the tourism industry is more advanced in the Mediterranean and Caribbean small island developing States than in those located in the Asia-Pacific and African regions. The two Mediterranean small island developing States, Cyprus and Malta, have experienced brisk expansion of tourism in the past, which is reflected by the high share of tourism in their GDP and their total foreign exchange earnings. In both of them, however, industry remains the dominant sector. The good performance of tourism in these countries is explained in part by their advantageous location in the vicinity of high-income European countries, particularly the United Kingdom of Great Britain and Northern Ireland, their main source market.

In the Caribbean, with a larger number of small island developing States, the pattern of economic performance has become closely linked to the performance of the tourism industry. The direct contribution of tourism in terms of its share in GDP and export earnings is high in most of them. In the wider Caribbean, travel and tourism is the largest relative contributor to the regional economy, at 31.5 per cent of GDP. While in some, the economic base is relatively diversified, in the majority of them most other activities have become increasingly linked to tourism, with agriculture and industry lagging behind. This is particularly the case in the smaller islands which have become essentially service economies. The development of tourism in the Caribbean has been helped by considerable amounts of foreign investments and the fact that they are located in the tropics but in proximity to high-income North America.

The level of development of tourism and its contribution to economic development is more uneven and generally much lower in small island developing States of the Asia-Pacific region than in those in the Mediterranean and Caribbean. In most of them, the level of general economic development is also much lower. Six of them - Maldives, Samoa, Vanuatu, Tuvalu, Kiribati, and Solomon Islands - are actually classified as least developed. Tourism activities are concentrated in only a few.

The contribution of tourism to national income is significant only in Fiji, Vanuatu, Samoa, Cook Islands and Maldives. By and large, in small island developing States of this region, agriculture and related activities predominate. Development of tourism in the region has been slow because of low levels of development of physical infrastructures and human resources in most of them, particularly the smaller ones, isolation from the major sources of tourists, problems of communal landownership, extremely weak aviation and communication links, and heavy reliance on foreign investment, with foreign investors concentrating on the most profitable destinations.

In the African region, considerable progress has been achieved in tourism development in Seychelles and

Mauritius. In the other three African small island developing States, Sao Tome and Principe, Cape Verde and the Comoros, all of which are classified as least developed, the development of tourism is still in an incipient stage. The slow pace of development of tourism in these countries is attributable to the slow pace of general economic development, and of the development of social and physical infrastructures and human resources in particular, as well as the inadequate importance attached to tourism as a growth sector in the past.

The future development of tourism in small island developing States will be affected by two principal current global trends. First, global travel and tourism is expected to grow more rapidly in the coming years, outpacing the growth of world economic output. Between 1995 and 2005, travel and tourism is projected to grow by an annual average rate of 5.5 per cent in real terms and create 12.5 million new direct and indirect jobs annually on the average.

In the wider Caribbean, travel and tourism output is projected to grow at an annual average rate of 3.6 per cent in real terms between 1995 and 2005 and to create 2.7 million jobs. For sustaining Caribbean tourism, the secretariat of the Caribbean Tourism Organization has identified a number of areas of action at the regional level, notably, maintenance of product quality, including the integrity of the natural environment; enhancement of profitability; provision of air access at competitive rates from major tourist markets; provision of a secure environment for the industry by combating crime and drugs; strengthening intersectoral linkages and creation of a regional competitive force through regional collaboration, particularly in the area of overseas marketing and promotion; and creation of social acceptability of the further expansion of tourism by the local population.

A similar trend is expected for Asia and the Pacific. The region as a whole is projected to be the fastest growing area in world tourism activities up to the year 2005. Between 1995 and 2005, the annual average real rate of growth of travel and tourism output in the region is estimated at 8.0 per cent. The South Pacific is expected to share in this growth through further growth of its traditional destinations, as well as through the gradual development of as yet untapped potentials in other islands.

In most of the small island developing States of the South Pacific, the growth of tourism will require the removal of several major internal constraints, including the following: shortages of trained staff; inadequacy and infrequency of air transportation; low level and quality of supporting infrastructure - airport facilities, tour operation, restaurants; low budgets for marketing and promotion; lack of investment capital; and restriction on landownership. By far the greatest challenge for the expansion of tourism in the South Pacific small island developing States will be their ability to achieve international competitiveness.

In the African region, Mauritius and Seychelles have planned for further growth but have opted for up-market tourism. They have consequently banned charter flight operations and hope to achieve a slower rate of growth of visitors, with emphasis on higher-spending visitors on scheduled flights.

Of particular concern to these countries is the spread of drugs and of diseases such as the human immunodeficiency virus/acquired immunodeficiency syndrome (HIV/AIDS), which can impact very severely on their small populations.

The other three African small island developing States have considerable room for growth and are just beginning to develop tourism as a growth sector.

In Malta and Cyprus, the rate of growth of tourist arrivals has slowed down in the recent past. This is attributable in part to capacity constraints and in part to deliberate policies to slow down expansion in order to deal with environmental and other adverse impacts of previous rapid expansion. Both countries plan to place considerable importance on tourism as a growth sector for quite some time to come, but have opted for up-market tourism.

A second discernible trend that will shape tourism development in small island developing States in coming years is the growing interest in and demand for specialty tourism. Underlying this trend is greater environmental awareness globally, greater health consciousness, and a growing preference by travellers to experience unspoilt environmental surroundings.

In tandem with this trend, many small island developing States have embarked on a gradual policy of diversification of the tourism package emphasizing to a greater extent other natural assets than the beach and the sea. Diversification of the tourism product also reflects the realization on the part of the authorities in small island developing States of the need to innovate in order to remain competitive.

Risks of over-reliance on tourism

Over-reliance on tourism, especially mass tourism, carries significant risks. Economic recession in industrialized countries, their major source of tourists, and the impacts of tropical storms and cyclones to which many of them are particularly prone have devastating effects on the tourism sector and hence on tourism-based island economies. Mass tourism, unlike up-market tourism, is characterized by relatively high income elasticity of demand and is likely to fall off suddenly as a result of economic recessions in the source markets. Excessive reliance on a single major source of tourists, as in Cyprus and Malta on the United Kingdom market, is extremely risky as economic difficulties in the source country have direct adverse impacts on the receiving countries.

In small islands, there is a tendency for fast growth of tourism to be accompanied by inflationary pressures. Prices of real estate, particularly land suitable for building, which is extremely scarce, quickly rise beyond the reach of the local population. Inflationary pressures build up throughout the economy as the prices of locally produced construction materials and consumer goods rise. Although this process means higher profit margins in bottleneck sectors and could stimulate more inward investment, overly accommodating monetary policy could generalize the inflation with adverse consequences for international competitiveness and future investment.

Social and Cultural Development

Sudden, rapid development of tourism can cause significant social disruptions in small island States. Pressures are exerted on households and communities by the upward pressure on land prices and prices of foodstuffs and household items. Among other things, potential long-run effects could be a reduction in the living standards of high proportions of island populations and a sense of alienation brought about by their lack of access to limited land resources.

Many small island populations also suffer a loss of access to beaches and important leisure areas because of exclusive rights granted to developers. This, in some cases, also translates into economic losses as fishermen and others are adversely affected by loss of access to the sea. Furthermore, excessively high visibility of foreigners can lead to anxieties on the part of the local people and a tendency to blame local problems on them, and thus to a social rejection of the growth of tourism.

An important factor in sustainable tourism development in small island States is the tourist carrying capacity of these societies, in both environmental and social terms. At peak periods, visitors are known to outnumber nationals by multiples in several of the smaller islands. In larger islands such as Jamaica or Fiji, local concentration of tourism often leads to localized problems of carrying capacity, such as overcrowding of beaches, traffic congestion, noise pollution, increased incidence of drugs and crime, and the spread of diseases brought in from outside.

While optimal carrying capacity cannot be quantified with any exactitude, it is generally contended that the population to tourists ratio, i.e., the inverse of what is shown in the table, should be kept at a level that does not exceed social tolerance limits, which may differ from country to country.

Island tourism is invariably centred on sun, sea and sand. However, to the extent that some interaction occurs with local customs and traditions, tourism is sometimes believed to exert a negative sociocultural influence on small island States. A high level of tourism can lead to commercialization, which is thought to cheapen local customs and traditions. Local arts and crafts and cultural practices are sometimes adapted to suit foreign tastes, which leads to the creation of contrived cultural products.

Some research conducted in the Asia-Pacific and Caribbean regions, however, has failed to produce much evidence of major destruction of local cultures as a result of the influence of tourists. On the contrary, the findings indicate that tourism can assist in preserving customs and cultures by providing incentives to invest in and promote them. If properly managed and promoted, local cultures can be given an impetus by the presence of tourists. It is contended, for instance, that the popularization of Jamaican reggae and carnival festivals of Trinidad and Tobago and similar cultural forms in other small island States is a direct result of the influence of tourism.

Environmental Development

The fragile ecosystems of small island States and their generally more limited scope for action in development alternatives make concerns for the environmental impact of tourism very acute, particularly because the sector, which is almost totally dependent on the natural environment, is viewed by many small island developing States as a fast route to social and economic development. Intensive tourism development and tourism activities often have very quick and severe impacts on their natural resources. The principal tourism-related environmental difficulties confronting small island developing States are several.

Land resources and terrestrial biological diversity

The environmental impacts of tourism are attributable to the development of tourism infrastructures and facilities and to the impacts of tourists' activities. In small islands, even more so than elsewhere, there is strong competition for the use of land between tourism and other competing uses. Rising prices of building land increase the pressure to build on agricultural land. Deforestation and intensified or unsuitable use of land cause erosion and loss of biological diversity. In many small island developing States, ecosystems are now being threatened as a result of the development of tourism, which has intensified human interference with vegetation and wildlife. This can lead to irreversible damage to their valuable ecosystems and to traditional activities such as fishing.

Waste management

For small island developing States, treatment and disposal of liquid and solid wastes constitute a major problem. With limited physical infrastructure, the capacity of many small island States is already strained. This is exacerbated by wastes generated by tourism activities. Examples abound of damages caused by the disposal of untreated effluents into surrounding areas of land and sea. Pollution of scarce inland freshwater resources is one such example. The loss of valuable marine life, the destruction of coral reefs and the silting and erosion of coastal beaches, on which island tourism highly depends, are others.

Pollution from ship-generated wastes is also a major cause for concern for small island developing States. One dimension of this particular threat is the dumping of oily waste, sewage, garbage and cargo residues, which cause marine and beach pollution, by merchant ships plying their seas. Another dimension, particularly for the Caribbean, is the frequency of tourist cruise ships plying that region's seas and generating substantial volumes of liquid and solid wastes for disposal at the ports of call. The following factors have been cited as impeding corrective action: inadequate infrastructure; weak institutional, legislative and enforcement capacities; the absence of a regional consensus on appropriate criteria for sewage, effluents and coastal water standards; and the inability of small island developing States to require cruise ships and other vessels to comply with the provisions of the International Convention for the Prevention of Pollution from Ships regarding generation and disposal of ship wastes.

Coastal area degradation

Tourism as a mainly coastal development has already had a number of adverse impacts on small island developing States. In Mauritius, Seychelles, Malta, Cyprus and several islands in the Caribbean, the previously unchecked construction of tourism facilities along their coastlines resulted in the despoliation of much of the originally pristine beauty of these areas.

In order to halt the degradation, the Governments of a number of these countries have, of late, taken steps through legislation to restrict and control coastal construction. Stipulations of building size, with limits on height and room capacity, and specifications of design and materials used in construction have been instituted in an effort to correct past errors and ensure better harmony with the natural environment. Beach destruction caused by intensive sand mining for tourism-related construction is also a feature of many coastal areas. This practice has recently been curtailed in Maldives, Seychelles, Mauritius, the Bahamas and Cook Islands, among other States.

Beaches destroyed by sand quarrying are not being naturally replenished because of the destruction of coral reefs by sewage and other types of pollution. Erosion owing to tourism facilities and infrastructures built too close to the coast also contributes to beach destruction and coastal degradation. Another common feature of coastal area destruction in small island developing States is the removal of valuable mangrove forests, which act as nesting places for birds and other animal life in addition to their function as a natural barrier against encroachment of the sea. Indiscriminate diving, fishing and boating activities associated with tourism may further contribute to this disturbance. For a detailed discussion of coastal area issues in small island developing States, see the report of the Secretary-General on coastal area management in small island developing States.

Freshwater Resources

The problem of freshwater availability is most severe in the low-lying atolls that have the least opportunity for surface-water catchment and storage. Several other small island developing States also suffer from frequent droughts and chronic water scarcity. On the high volcanic islands, rainfall is in many cases abundant but access to freshwater is often limited by lack of adequate storage facilities and delivery systems. The supply of freshwater relative to the growing demand from agriculture, industry and households is becoming an acute problem in many small island developing States. Added to this is the growing competition of limited water resources from tourism, which is extremely water-intensive.

Climate change and sealevel rise

Island tourism is a climate-sensitive industry, and being largely concentrated in coastal locations is susceptible to sealevel rise. An analysis of data by the Intergovernmental Panel on Climate Change has confirmed a trend in global warming, with increases in temperatures of 0.3 to 0.6 degrees centigrade occurring since the late nineteenth century, much of which has occurred in the past 40 years. The effect of this trend is a rise of mean sealevels at a rate of 1.5 millimetres per year. In small islands and coastal areas in general, that would cause the inundation of coastal and some inland areas, threatening sanitation systems and freshwater supplies as seawater infiltrates subterranean water tables, with possibly catastrophic consequences for island tourism.

An erosion of shorelines would undoubtedly bring about severe stress and damage to both natural and built environments, the overall economic consequences of which are currently inestimable. In addition, damages from tropical storms with a possible link to changes in weather patterns have been increasing in recent years. Small island developing States that are especially vulnerable to these phenomena now experience considerable difficulty securing insurance coverage. Reliable sunshine is one of the major tourism assets of tropical islands. Potential threats of climate change, which are beginning to appear in greater health risks from direct exposure to sunlight, may undermine this asset.

Policy Issues

The present section discusses some of the main policy issues in the area of sustainable development of tourism at the national, regional and international levels. Emphasis is placed on legislation, finance, capacity-building, and sustainable tourism infrastructure and policies as necessary means of implementing the provisions of the Programme of Action.

National level

Development policy framework

Tourism development has been incorporated into the overall development plans of some small islands. Some Caribbean island authorities have established tourism master plans, with links to national development plans, and have created national sustainable development commissions or, as in the case of Saint Lucia, a National Sustainable Tourism Commission.

In the South Pacific, tourism development plans and policies have been formulated in several small island developing States. However, the level of policy commitment to sustainable tourism development differs from country to country, which in turn influences the degree of action in this area. According to a study by the Economic and Social Commission for Asia and the Pacific (ESCAP), this uneven commitment in the South Pacific can serve as an impediment to the promotion of sustainability at the regional level.

By and large, a long-term national policy for sustainable tourism development, with emphasis on natural resource conservation, has yet to evolve. The focus of policies generally continues to be on:

(a) creating and improving conditions for attracting foreign investment in tourism;

(b) marketing and promotion of tourism to achieve maximum growth in arrivals; and

(c) designing the type of legislative framework that would further those objectives.

The prevalence of this situation points to the urgent need for a policy framework for sustainable tourism development in most small island developing States.

Legislative framework

A necessary requirement for the pursuit of sustainable tourism development is an effective legislative framework. A wide range of laws have been enacted in small island developing States, in many instances since the conclusion of the United Nations Conference on Environment and Development, establishing standards for land use in tourism development, tourism facilities and investment in tourism.

Despite progress in the enactment of environmental legislation, its effectiveness continues to be impaired by weaknesses in the institutional frameworks for enforcing legislation, lack of standardization of legislation and the obscurity of regulations. Consequently, the level of enforcement of regulations to ensure sustainability in tourism in many small island developing States leaves much to be desired. Regulations for coastal zone management and the creation of protected areas, both marine and land-based, present a case in point. Their enforcement, particularly in the Caribbean, remains very weak.

Investment

The majority of small island developing States suffer from a lack of local capital for bulky investments and, in many cases, the absence of a significant local entrepreneurial class. The financing required for the development of the tourism sector is therefore obtained largely through foreign investment. Special efforts are made by Governments of small island developing States to attract foreign capital through the provision of tax breaks, tax holidays, building concessions and other incentives to foreign investors. While that may well be necessary to some extent, competition among small island developing States to attract foreign capital for tourism development often leads to the provision of over-generous financial incentives to foreign investors which deprive all these States of part of the income from tourism.

Moreover, since small island developing States are over-reliant on foreign capital, they are unable to impose environmental sustainability conditions on foreign investors. Both to derive the maximum benefits from tourism and to avoid environmental deterioration from tourism activities, there is a need for small island developing States to jointly adopt uniform incentive and environmental policies, at least at the regional level.

While efforts at encouraging local investment and participation in the sector have increased in many small island developing States, considerably more effort is needed. Such efforts are, in many cases, hampered by the inability of the private sector in most small island developing States to raise adequate capital. A judicious mix of foreign and local investment, and especially the encouragement of joint ventures, would be one way of ensuring the adequacy of capital resources for sustainable tourism development and the fuller participation of nationals in the sector.

Aside from foreign direct investment in tourism, the bulk of tourism-related services are also known to be largely in the control of foreign operators in a number of small island developing States. Overseas sales and marketing, and promotion of tourism packages for most small island developing States, are undertaken by outside entities. Several domestic operations are also handled by foreigners.

In this area, there is a need for increased investments in the training of nationals for greater participation in tourism.

In order to supplement the efforts of the private sector at ensuring sustainability in the tourism sector, greater non-governmental organization/government partnerships in tourism development could be developed. Such partnerships can be useful, especially in the restoration, development and maintenance of cultural and historical sites, while ensuring conservation and profitability.

Funds for investment in such activities could be raised through mechanisms already existing in many cases, such as increases in airport taxes and airline ticket taxes, as long as they meet International Civil Aviation Organization (ICAO) stipulations, and entrance fees for tourism sites.

Human and institutional capacity

Most small island States face the persistent problem of inadequate supply of trained manpower, particularly in government agencies responsible for the implementation and monitoring of standards and environmental regulations in tourism. The shortage of skilled human resources is compounded by the dispersion in some States of roles and responsibilities among several government agencies. To address these weaknesses, an integrated approach to tourism planning and environmental conservation, coupled with training at all levels, needs immediate attention in all small island States.

A system for monitoring the implementation of sustainable tourism policies must also form part of an integrated approach to tourism planning and the building up of institutional capacity. A study by ESCAP found that national tourism organizations, important mechanisms in the development and implementation of sustainable tourism policies, are largely under-staffed and under-funded.

The study also found that attempts by individual small island States to market their tourism product themselves have not been significantly effective in most cases because of the high costs involved and the lack of skilled human resources. Overall, the shortcomings of capacity could be better addressed through greater regional collaboration.

Infrastructure

The main physical infrastructural requirements for tourism development include the following:

— effective transportation facilities, including airports and air and/or sea carrier links;
— reasonably good road networks;
— telecommunication links;
— reliable energy supply systems;
— freshwater supply systems;
— accommodation facilities;
— restaurants and entertainment sites.

For many small island developing States, the inadequacy of these infrastructures is an obstacle to the development of the sector. In some of the smaller Pacific islands in this category, efforts are being made to build new airport facilities. This is regarded as a necessary initial step to their fuller participation in tourism. In the Caribbean, where the sector is more developed, air links to long-haul markets such as Germany, Italy and France are being extended.

Many small island developing States are confronted with severe infrastructural inadequacies consequent to the growth of tourism. Many of them suffer from chronic shortages of freshwater supply for their own use, a problem that is further aggravated by the high demand of large tourist populations. Liquid and solid waste disposal present a colossal problem to all small island developing States but especially to those that are tourism-based. Another dimension is added to this problem by the requirement of facilities to handle waste brought to their ports by cruise lines which frequent small island destinations.

The diversification of the tourism product through the development of nature and cultural tourism also necessitates additional infrastructural and environmental requirements. Some sites are remote and may require additional access routes and other infrastructures such as those for the supply of water and electricity, and new accommodation. These requirements are particularly burdensome to the archipelagic small island developing States. Generally, when developing infrastructure, the issue of the carrying capacity of the destination must also be considered.

Technology

Sector-specific technology needs of small island developing States are discussed in various reports to the Commission on Sustainable Development at its fourth session which highlight the need for the introduction or more widespread use of certain technologies by tourism enterprises and Governments of small island developing States, as appropriate. Some examples are:

(a) solar technology for cooling of hotels and for water heating;

(b) environmentally sound technologies for the treatment, recycling and disposal of solid wastes generated by tourism facilities and those brought to port by cruise ships;

(c) telecommunications technologies for the fuller integration of small island developing States into global telecommunications networks to enhance their marketing and promotion operations; and

(d) electronic information technologies to enhance day-to-day tourism operations, such as reservations.

Regional level

The need for greater collaboration among small island developing States on issues of sustainable tourism development is well recognized. Collaboration and cooperation could lead to greater long-term benefits for the environment and the economies of small island developing States, particularly in an increasingly competitive global arena.

The harmonization of standards and regulations, including legislative actions to govern tourism, has been identified as a critical need in the Programme of Action for the Sustainable Development of Small Island Developing States and by some regional authorities. Integrated tourism development planning, marketing and promotion can increase both effectiveness and efficiency. Joint overseas marketing and promotion would help achieve benefits of economies of scale and increased value-added in the tourism sector. Overseas marketing and promotion by individual small island developing States entail a heavy cost to each of these States and reduce significantly their net foreign exchange earnings from tourism.

The Programme of Action provides for the pursuit of regional initiatives in:

(a) the harmonization of standards and regulations to ensure that tourism and the environment are mutually supportive;

(b) the promotion of cooperation in developing potential complementarities in the tourism sector; and

(c) the establishment of mechanisms for information exchange and sharing of experiences, particularly through existing regional tourism organizations.

The ESCAP report cited above has identified, in addition to those measures, the need for regional collaboration in:

(a) integrating tourism development planning, including concerted market development and promotion;

(b) strengthening and expanding the roles of national and regional tourism institutions and organs; and

(c) promoting joint training and manpower development in tourism.

In recent years, attempts have been made, particularly in the two main regions - the Pacific and the Caribbean - to consolidate efforts in sustainable tourism development by forging common regional approaches for the sector. The necessary institutional framework currently exists for these regions in the form of the Tourism Council of the South Pacific and the Caribbean Tourism Organization. These institutions have been mandated by the respective regional political forums - the South Pacific Forum and the Caribbean Community (CARICOM) - to strengthen regional cooperation in tourism development, planning and promotion. Provision for some financial support has been made for both institutions under the Caribbean and Pacific regional tourism development programmes funded by the Lome' Convention concluded between the European Community and the African, Caribbean and Pacific States.

In spite of many difficulties, the Tourism Council of the South Pacific has been successful as a regional agency in the area of marketing and promotion of the South Pacific as a tourist destination, but not in the area of strategy and planning. For the Caribbean small island developing States, the political framework was consolidated with the formation in 1995 of the Association of Caribbean States (ACS), which has identified the tourism sector as one of three areas for high-priority measures for wider regional cooperation. Regional cooperation in the area of tourism has been further strengthened by the formation of the Caribbean Coalition for Tourism, with the goal of creating the largest possible pool of resources for cooperative marketing by drawing on the resources of the widest range of players both in the public and in the private sectors.

Resource constraint has been recognized as an impediment for both TCSP and CTO to adequately cover the broad range of activities that they must undertake to increase market awareness, promote sustainability, develop human resources and carry out marketing and promotion. External assistance is seen as essential to the viability of both institutions. Increased support for these bodies, aside from regional Governments, will be contingent upon increased involvement of the private sector in their work. The inadequacy of political will to cooperate meaningfully is also seen as a major impediment to effective cooperation in both regions.

In the African region, there is little evidence of meaningful effort at regional cooperation in the area of tourism development. This may be due in large part to the dispersion of the African small island developing States, three off the east coast and two off the west coast of Africa, and the considerable disparity in development and policy emphasis on tourism among these countries. Given the recognized potential for tourism development, however, there is a need to begin efforts within this region for a common approach to sustainable tourism development through an integrated subregional policy.

In the areas of joint training and manpower development, tourism research and experience-sharing efforts at regional collaboration have been made to varying extents within the regions. The pooling within each region of the limited financial and technical resources of individual small island developing States for capacity-building would be immensely beneficial to all those States. Collaboration in information exchange and research could be achieved through the strengthening of regional tourism institutions. A priority need in this respect is for training in the use of state-of-the-art information technologies at the regional level for the monitoring of environmental impacts of tourism, and for the establishment and operation of central reservation systems.

A major area for regional cooperation is air transportation. Two considerations are worthy of note in this connection. First, small island developing States cannot depend solely on foreign carriers, which must make decisions in the best interest of their owners regarding services, routes and schedules. Such decisions may not always coincide with the best interest of the countries. Besides, even a major airline serving small island developing States in a region can suddenly disappear. Secondly, small island developing States, except for a few, cannot each maintain a viable airline. An effective solution from the point of view of cost and adequacy of air transportation for the tourism industry would be regionally owned and managed carriers, with provision for regional functional cooperation. For a detailed discussion on air transport needs for small island developing States, see the report of the Secretary- General on air transport in small island developing States.

COUTRY EXPERIENCES

The economic prospects of many small island developing States depend significantly on a productive tourism sector. For the States, generally, the furtherance of sustainable tourism development is an economic as well as a socio-environmental imperative. In these countries, tourism actually provides an economic rationale for safeguarding the natural environment.

Many of the policies that underpin sustainable development were recognized and elaborated in a number of small island developing States prior to the United Nations Conference on Environment and Development and were given further impetus by it and by the Barbados Conference. For instance, Maldives, concerned about sustainability in the wake of rapid tourism development, recognized the need for the establishment of a National Environment Council to address those concerns as far back as 1985.

The preparation of a national environment action programme, as well as a related work programme, was completed in 1989, with provision for the systematic inclusion of environmental issues in the country's national development plan. Specific policies have been adopted to promote sustainable tourism development, particularly in the areas of waste disposal, use of coral reefs and construction in coastal sites and for the type and diversity of accommodation.

Policies aimed at the creation of national parks and the encouragement of visits to wildlife refuges, bird sanctuaries and other natural beauty spots have been put in place in Seychelles and Mauritius as a means of diversifying the tourism product with a possible spin-off benefit for the protection and conservation of these sites. The drive for product diversification and the enhancement of natural endowments is also very strong in the Caribbean.

Several legislative acts have been passed in individual countries of this region with the objective of addressing environmental problems. For example, in Saint Lucia, a National Sustainable Tourism Commission was established and a National Environmental Action Plan was prepared for implementation in 1994. A Minimum Standards Act was scheduled for adoption in 1995, with a view to addressing all areas of hotel, restaurant and tourist carrying capacity.

A Development Control Act has also been approved by the Saint Lucia authorities, making the conduct of environmental impact assessment and its incorporation into all decision-making processes mandatory. Jamaica recently carried out a review of existing environmental legislation. The review resulted in the passage of new legislation requiring the conduct of environmental impact assessment for all new developments.

In some small island developing States where rapid tourism expansion has given rise to problems of sustainability and over-reliance on tourism as a major sector, several measures have been taken in an attempt to overcome such problems. A case in point is Cyprus, where pollution, beach erosion, physical carrying capacity and difficulties of competitive pressures on other economic sectors have been felt. Efforts have been made through the use of economic instruments and legislation to achieve sustainability and balance.

Various new tax incentives have been introduced to diversify and upgrade the tourism product and a new marketing strategy focus is directed at improving tourist quality. Additionally, fiscal instruments are now being used to encourage sound land use and coastal zone practices aimed particularly at slowing down and improving coastal development and efficient allocation and use of water and other resources. Simultaneously, a policy of economic restructuring in the manufacturing and agriculture sectors have been put in place in order to improve their overall competitiveness and linkages with tourism.

Diversification within or away from tourism has been undertaken in many small island developing States, notably in Cyprus and Malta. Several constraining factors have been recognized, including a generally limited scope and capacity for novel forms of tourism development in small islands, a usually small proportion of visitors interested in other forms of activity, and more importantly, the fact that all aspects of tourism accommodation and other facilities have been geared towards traditional forms of tourism.

The authorities in Mauritius and Seychelles have also adopted some policies for diversification within tourism, particularly in targeting high-spending visitors and in encouraging to some extent inland and nature tourism. In the foreseeable future, however, the need for continued mass tourism is acknowledged largely because of an existing over-capacity in tourism.

A spin-off benefit of the thrust for quality has been a general upgrading of facilities and greater attention to avoiding negative impacts. Mauritius has been relatively successful in achieving some degree of economic diversification and balanced growth through the development of export processing zones and, to a lesser extent, agricultural modernization and diversification.

In the Comoros and Cape Verde, the Governments and private sector have recently demonstrated heightened interest in tourism development. The institutional groundwork has been prepared in the Comoros with the adoption in 1994 of a national environmental policy document and an environmental plan of action, and the creation in 1995 of the Association Touristique Comorienne.

The implementation of these plans, however, is subject to a number of constraints, including poor levels of infrastructure development, particularly hotels, poor air and communication links with tourist-generating areas and some degree of political instability. Recent initiatives in Cape Verde include the adoption of a tourism development plan and the establishment of a National Institute for Tourism. The main constraints identified are the following: a lack of interest by the local and foreign private sector; a lack of demonstrated support by donors for the tourism development plan; and limited domestic financial resources.

Dominica has formally launched eco-tourism as the main form of tourism development. The island is mountainous, boasts few beaches but has 60 per cent forest cover containing many endemic species of plants, animals and birds. Two large national parks, two forest reserves and a Carib Indian reservation form the basis of eco-tourism attractions. The Government of Dominica has enacted legislation to ensure heritage and natural resource preservation, and the creation of linkages with local economic activities.

While no scientific assessment has been conducted of the impact of increased human activity on the natural environment, several negative trends have been observed, among which are the accumulation of litter and garbage around nature sites, the extraction of plants from protected areas and the effects of the use of soap by local people in rivers and natural pools. Based on the experience of Dominica, concerns have been expressed regarding issues of carrying capacity and the impact of large numbers of tourists on environmentally sensitive ecologies.

Although the adoption of regulations and policy guidelines can be seen as an indication of government commitment to sustainability, weaknesses persist in the management and policing of protected areas and tourism sites. Another unique feature of the experience of Dominica is the emphasis on participation by the local population through tax exemptions for local shareholder participation in hotels and other ventures.

Role of International NGO in Promotiong Tourism Development in Small Islands

Private sector

A survey conducted by the World Travel and Tourism Council indicates that in much of the private sector, the pursuit of sustainability measures in tourism is gradually becoming a matter of sound business practice. Little by little, recognition of the link between conservation measures on the one hand and profitability and competitiveness on the other is taking hold. Some private sector companies involved in travel and tourism have reported positive results from conservation measures, in the form of increased profitability, a rise in staff morale and an enhanced image among their clientele.

In order to develop voluntary practice approaches, tourism industry associations have emphasized the use of voluntary environmental codes of conduct and guidelines. Through a survey and publication, the United Nations Environment Programme (UNEP)/Industry and Environment Programme Activities Centre has identified more than 30 codes, among them, those prepared by main industry associations such as the World Travel and Tourism Council, the Pacific Asia Travel Association, the American Society of Travel and the International Hotels Environment Initiative.

An emerging feature among some multinational businesses, particularly in the hotel sector, is resort to voluntary measures for conservation, primarily with a view to securing strategic advantages, but also as a means of precluding more costly retrofitting that may be required by future government regulations. However, to date, most efforts have focused on energy and water conservation, waste minimization and product purchase. New tourism developments should more often incorporate improved plant designs, and improved energy-efficient features that will enable greater natural lighting, natural cooling of accommodation facilities, and waste treatment and water recycling.

Already, some progress can be noted: hotel staff are being trained to adopt energy- and water-saving, and waste-minimization measures during cleaning; and hotel guests are being encouraged to minimize water use by the reuse of towels and linens. Product purchase measures are being instituted, for example, through switching from phosphate-free cleaning products to those known to have less harmful properties.

In the Asia-Pacific region, the development of integrated resorts is setting a new trend in resort development with the key objective of exercising greater control over environmental quality as a means of providing a guarantee of quality to guests. New complexes are built with all facilities on site, with particular emphasis on water conservation and recycling, energy supply and conservation, and waste management.

NGOs and community involvement

The growing trend of environmental awareness globally is accompanied by an increase in international and national environmental movements in tourism development. For instance, at the international level, the International Scientific Council for Island Development, with the support of the Government of Spain and the sponsorship of several organizations, spearheaded the convening of the World Conference on Sustainable Tourism at Lanzarote, Canary Islands, in April 1995. The Conference adopted a Charter for Sustainable Tourism which affirms, inter alia, that:

(a) tourism must be sustainable and integrated with the natural, cultural and human environment;

(b) the achievement of sustainability is contingent upon integrated planning and cooperation at all levels;

(c) tourism development must contribute to local economic development and improve the quality of life of all people; and

(d) the benefits and burdens of tourism must be more equitably distributed.

In consequence of the Conference, a follow-up committee responsible for the dissemination of the Charter and for the promotion of related studies, projects and actions was established; and the launching of a European network for sustainable tourism development in islands and coastal zones was proposed. The objective of the network is to generate and diffuse information and know-how on the promotion of environmentally sound tourism.

Like industry associations, non-governmental organizations such as the Ecotourism Society and the World Wide Fund for Nature Tourism Concern have also developed codes of conduct and guidelines for tourism. At the regional level, the Caribbean Conference on Sustainable Tourism, which was held at Punta Cana, Dominican Republic, towards the end of 1995, under the sponsorship of Earthkind International and the Earth Pledge Foundation, explored a wide range of issues relating to sustainable tourism in that region. A similar conference is planned for the South Pacific in 1996.

At the local level, the involvement of non-governmental organizations, community groups and local authorities in the promotion and development of sustainable tourism policies is just beginning but a discernible trend is apparent in some small island developing States.

The following are examples of recent initiatives: in Trinidad and Tobago, a project has been put in place at Matura Beach to train community youths as tour guides, with the goal of preventing poaching of leatherback turtles, an endangered species; in Jamaica, resort boards, which include representatives of non-governmental organizations, the local community and business enterprises, have been established in the main tourism areas of Ocho Rios, Montego Bay, Negril and Port Antonio for overseeing all aspects of tourism policy, practice and development; in Mauritius, the authorities have published The Mauritian

Code of Ethics for Tourism: For Mauritians. The Code, which focuses largely on the social and cultural aspects of tourism, presents guidelines for use by the local community in their dealings with tourists.

Role of UN Bodies

A number of organizations and bodies of the United Nations system have reported plans and activities in the area of tourism development, in keeping with the Programme of Action. The United Nations Development Programme has reported that its programme of assistance in the South Pacific and in some small island developing States in the other regions addresses issues relating to sustainable tourism development within the overall national environmental plans of the countries concerned.

The Economic Commission for Latin America and the Caribbean (ECLAC) and ESCAP have planned or recently implemented specific activities in tourism. ECLAC has reported that proposals for environmental codes of conduct for the tourism sector, which it recently developed, are now being carried out by the Caribbean Tourism Organization. ESCAP has reported that in 1995, it convened a workshop on integrated tourism planning in Pacific island countries and published a set of studies on foreign investment in the tourism sector in Samoa and Vanuatu.

The United Nations University is currently undertaking a study to examine indicators of sustainability for the tourism sector in small islands, along with a project on eco-tourism. It is expected that the results of these two undertakings will be useful to small island developing States.

In 1992-1993, the World Heritage Convention, sponsored by the United Nations Educational, Scientific and

Cultural Organization (UNESCO), in collaboration with UNEP, carried out surveys on tourism management in natural and mixed heritage sites and subsequently convened an international seminar which helped formulate a set of general principles for tourism development in natural heritage sites.

During 1994-1995, UNESCO collaborated with several regional initiatives on tourism in the Asia-Pacific region. The Earth Sciences Division of UNESCO has undertaken modelling of human-induced geomorphologic change to serve as a guide to improved planning of human settlements. In addition, UNESCO has planned a world heritage promotion seminar for the Caribbean, and a pilot project on water supply problems and community attitudes in the South Pacific islands, as well as studies with reference to the Caribbean on the interrelationships between tourism, population pressures, pollution and natural hazards.

In 1993, through the Pan American Health Organization Regional Office, the World Health Organization collaborated with a number of regional organizations to launch the Environmental Health and Sustainable Tourism Development Initiative for the Caribbean and to convene the Regional Conference on Environmental Health and Sustainable Development in the Caribbean.

UNEP is making efforts to promote integrated coastal zone management in small island developing States through its regional seas programme. The Mediterranean Action Plan and the Caribbean Action Plan have in particular addressed tourism issues. The Industry and Environment Office of UNEP has developed fruitful partnerships with industry associations at the international level to inform about and disseminate examples of good environmental practices, in particular on codes of conduct and environment management of hotels. The Food and Agriculture Organization of the United Nations has planned two regional workshops in 1996, one for the Caribbean and one for the South Pacific small island developing States. One of the items on the agenda of both workshops will be linkages of tourism with agriculture, forestry and fisheries.

Role of Other intergovernmental bodies

In addition to the Tourism Council of the South Pacific and the Caribbean Tourism Organization, both of which are intergovernmental bodies whose activities have been discussed above, the Organization of American States (OAS) and the European Union have been active in promoting sustainable tourism development in small island developing States. OAS has assisted Caribbean small island developing States in various policy studies on sustainable tourism. The European Union has provided assistance, under ongoing cooperation arrangements, in carrying out a number of tourism development projects in African, Caribbean and Pacific small island developing States.

Future Trends

Tourism already makes an important contribution to economic growth, employment and foreign exchange earnings in the majority of small island developing States. It provides an opportunity to most of them for economic diversification and growth.

Looking to the future, there are indications that the development of tourism in small island developing States will be subject to two current global trends.

First, global travel and tourism output is expected to grow more rapidly in coming years, outpacing the growth of world economic output. This trend is expected to reinforce current trends in small island developing States.

Secondly, tourism development in these countries will be shaped by the growing interest in, and demand for, specialty tourism, particularly nature tourism propelled by growing environmental awareness. To these trends may be added another, namely, an apparent upward trend in global warming and sealevel rise, the persistence of which would have devastating impacts on island tourism.

From the point of view of the future course of action, the following findings on the economic, social and environmental aspects of tourism in small island developing States are worthy of note:

a) *Economic aspects*

(i) the leakages through imports out of direct tourist expenditures to meet the needs of the tourism sector itself are extremely high in these countries;

(ii) the daily expenditures per visitor vary from country to country but are generally low;

(iii) excessive reliance on tourism carries many risks, including excessive exposure to international economic shocks and weakening of intersectoral linkages which, inter alia, reduce the potential benefits from tourism;

b) *Social aspects.* Rapid development of tourism, particularly mass tourism, can have significant adverse social impacts in small islands. The following are of particular significance:

(i) persistent inflationary pressures pose the danger of significantly worsening the household distribution of income;

(ii) the social carrying capacity of small islands quickly reaches its limits of tolerance as the ratio of visitors to the local population rises, causing overcrowding of beaches, noise pollution and exacerbating traffic congestion;

(iii) prolonged growth of mass tourism may be accompanied by increased incidence of crime, and spread of drugs and diseases, including HIV/AIDS;

(c) *Environmental aspects*. Intensive tourism development and tourism activities, particularly if not properly planned and managed, can very quickly cause environmental damages in small island developing States. The most notable impacts are observable in:

(i) land degradation and loss of terrestrial and marine biodiversity;

(ii) increased levels of pollution from dumping of solid and liquid wastes generated by tourism activities on land and in the sea;

(iii) coastal zone degradation through intensive sand mining, removal of mangrove forests and destruction of coral reefs, erosion and destruction of landscape owing to tourism facilities and associated infrastructures;

(iv) freshwater shortages aggravated by the demand from the water-intensive tourism industry, excessive groundwater pumping and consequent lowering of water tables.

Declaration of Barbaods

We the States participating in the Global Conference on the Sustainable Development of Small Island Developing States,

Having met in Bridgetown, Barbados from 25 April to 6 May 1994,

Reaffirming the principles and commitments to sustainable development embodied in the Rio Declaration on Environment and Development, Agenda 21 and the Non-legally Binding Authoritative Statement of Principles for a Global Consensus on the Management, Conservation and Sustainable Development of All Types of Forests, which were adopted by the nations of the world at the United Nations Conference on Environment and Development on 14 June 1992, as well as in the United Nations Framework Convention on Climate Change and the Convention on Biological Diversity,

Recognizing that the Global Conference on the Sustainable Development of Small Island Developing States translates Agenda 21 into specific policies, actions and measures to be taken at the national, regional and international levels to enable small island developing States to achieve sustainable development,

Part One

Affirm that:

I

1. The survival of small island developing States is firmly rooted in their human resources and cultural heritage,

which are their most significant assets; those assets are under severe stress and all efforts must be taken to ensure the central position of people in the process of sustainable development.

2. Sustainable development programmes must seek to enhance the quality of life of peoples, including their health, well-being and safety.

3. Full attention should be given to gender equity and to the important role and contribution of women, as well as to the needs of women and other major groups, including children, youth and indigenous people.

II

Small island developing States have sovereign rights over their own natural resources. Their biodiversity is among the most threatened in the world and their ecosystems provide ecological corridors linking major areas of biodiversity around the world. They bear responsibility for a significant portion of the world's oceans and seas and their resources. The efforts of small island developing States to conserve, protect and restore their ecosystems deserve international cooperation and partnership.

III

1. Small island developing States are particularly vulnerable to natural as well as environmental disasters and have a limited capacity to respond to and recover from such disasters.

2. While small island developing States are among those that contribute least to global climate change and

sealevel rise, they are among those that would suffer most from the adverse effects of such phenomena and could in some cases become uninhabitable. Therefore, they are among those particularly vulnerable States that need assistance under the United Nations Framework Convention on Climate Change, including adaptation measures and mitigation efforts.

3. Small island developing States share with all nations a critical interest in the protection of coastal zones and oceans against the effects of land-based sources of pollution.

4. Limited freshwater resources, increasing amounts of waste and hazardous substances, and limited facilities for waste disposal combine to make pollution prevention, waste management and the transboundary movement of hazardous materials critical issues for small island developing States.

IV

Small island developing States are limited in size, have vulnerable economies and are dependent both upon narrow resource bases and on international trade, without the means of influencing the terms of that trade.

V

To enhance their national capacities and self-reliance, small island developing States, with the assistance and support of the international community, should actively promote human resources development programmes including education, training and skills development. Their institutional and administrative capacity to implement the programme of action must be strengthened at all levels by supportive partnerships and cooperation, including technical assistance, the further development of legislation and mechanisms for information sharing.

VI

There is an urgent need in small island developing States to address the constraints to sustainable development, including scarce land resources, which lead to difficult land and agriculture use decisions; limited fresh water; education and training needs; health and human settlement requirements; inordinate pressures on coastal and marine environment and resources; and limited means available to exploit natural resources on a sustainable basis.

VII

1. The special role of non-governmental organizations and the importance of a partnership between Governments, intergovernmental organizations and agencies, non-governmental organizations and other major groups in implementing Agenda 21 and the programme of action at the national, subregional, regional and international levels should be recognized.
2. That partnership should include efforts to increase public awareness of the outcomes and follow-up of the Global Conference on the Sustainable Development of Small Island Developing States through all available means of communication.

PART TWO

Declare that:

I

Based on the principle of the right to development, small island developing States should, in accordance with their own priorities, endeavour to achieve the goals of sustainable development by, inter alia, formulating and implementing policies, strategies and programmes that take into account development, health and environmental goals, strengthening national institutions, and mobilizing all available resources, all of which are aimed at improving the quality of life.

II

Through regional and subregional cooperation, small island developing States and the international community should encourage strong functional cooperation in the promotion of sustainable development by sharing information and technology, strengthening institutions and building capacity.

III

1. The international community should cooperate with small island developing States in the implementation of the Programme of Action for the Sustainable Development of Small Island Developing States by providing effective means, including adequate, predictable new and additional financial resources in

accordance with chapter 33 of Agenda 21; facilitating the transfer of environmentally sound technology, including on concessional and preferential terms as mutually agreed, taking into account the need to protect intellectual property rights as well as the special needs of developing countries; and promoting fair, equitable and non-discriminatory trading arrangements and a supportive international economic system.

2. The international community has a responsibility to facilitate the efforts of small island developing States to minimize the stress on their fragile ecosystems, including through cooperative action and partnership.
3. To achieve sustainable development and a higher quality of life for all people, including people of small island developing States, all States should reduce and eliminate unsustainable patterns of production and consumption, and should promote appropriate demographic policies.
4. The international community should build new and equitable partnerships for the sustainable development of small island developing States through the implementation of the Programme of Action and should send a powerful message to the world's peoples on the possibilities of joint action undertaken with a sense of common purpose and partnership.

HAINAN DECLARATION

Islands differ greatly in size, climate, terrain, biodiversity, access, and in human history, habitation, culture, land tenure, legal systems and economic activity, including tourism.

For many islands of the Asia-Pacific Region, tourism is the main economic activity, in terms of both income and employment generation. Due to their relatively small size, islands are quite vulnerable from both an environmental and a social point of view. This vulnerability may put at risk the long-term sustainability of tourism-based economic development of the islands, if tourism is not appropriately planned, developed and managed.

The Conference on Sustainable Tourism in the Island of the Asia-Pacific Region, as the previous one held in Capri, Italy, for Mediterranean Islands in May 2000, was intended as a regional follow up to the WTO/UNEP Conference on Sustainable Tourism in Small Island Developing States and Other Islands, held in Lanzarote, Spain 1998.

The aim of the Conference was to examine the various aspects that need to be considered by governments and the private sector if they wish tourism to contribute to the overall economic, social and environmental sustainability of their territories. This means developing a tourism infrastructure and a tourism industry that are sustainable in the long term, maximising the social and economic benefits and reducing the negative impacts on the environment.

The Hainan Conference was convened from December 6 to 8, 2000, in the Gloria Resort in Sanya, organised by WTO and UNEP, and with the support of UNESCO, the China National Tourism Administration and the Hainan Provincial government. Over 100 participants from 23 countries in the Asia-Pacific region, and representatives of

7 inter-governmental organizations, agreed to the following conclusions, as:

Critical Issues for Sustainable Island Tourism Development in the Asia and Pacific Region:

1 There is no other economic activity that cuts across so many sectors, levels and interests as tourism. There is a vital need, therefore to integrate planning for tourism with national development and resource management plans.

Stakeholders:

2 Sustainable tourism in Asia-Pacific islands requires effective partnerships between the governments, tourism industry, landholders and land managers, and local communities.

3 Governments play a critical role through their institutional leadership, guaranteeing stakeholders' participation. The Governments' role is also essential in the establishment of regulatory and policy frameworks, ensuring their enforcement, the application of appropriate economic instruments (including the removal of environmentally perverse subsidies), and monitoring environmental quality.

4 The private sector provides the expertise to establish, market and operate economically sustainable tourism enterprises. The tourism industry has a critical role in the development, promotion and adoption of environmentally appropriate technologies,

management practices, planning and land use (including site selection), marketing (including eco-labeling) and the education of the tourists. When planning tourism, consideration should be given to cater for each particular group/market segment that is considered appropriate for the type of products offered. Where necessary, promotional brochures should allocate reasonable space to producing information about the country's social, cultural and environmental resources.

5 Landholders, protected area managers and environmental *NGOs* maintain the environmental integrity of the natural resource and natural attractions.

6 Local communities maintain cultural identity and social fabrics, and provide local cultural opportunities for tourists and local economic opportunities for residents. One of the failures of tourism planning in the past has been the lack of attention given to local populations who are not consulted regarding decisions which have long term direct impacts on their lives and futures.

7 It is important therefore that **local people** understand that they are the primary stakeholders in the expansion and maintenance of a successful tourism industry. That understanding will require ongoing community participation and educational programmes at all levels that explain the role of tourism vis-à-vis the environment and the economy. More importantly, it is the direct knowledge that they are participating in the environmental conservation of the country (and globally) and benefiting economically from tourism.

Sensitive areas:

8 Particular conditions apply for tourism in World Heritage and other protected areas. Tourism in these areas should occur only in compliance with a management plan which recognises the conservation of heritage values as the primary land management goal, and which includes environmental assessment, effective monitoring of environmental as well as social and economic indicators, and continuous assessment of the success or otherwise of visitor and resource management tools and actions.

9 As a further tool for resource management, zoning within these areas can indicate where tourism may be permitted and physical development located and, even more important, where it may not be located.

Other issues:

10 Responsible energy and water use is fundamental to sustainable development and a sustainable future. A broad range of those sustainable technology and management alternatives is available – tourism planners in developing countries in the Asia Pacific Region need more access to it. One way of achieving this technology transfer is through web based networks and exchange mechanisms.

11 A global programme of 'greening' tourism accommodation and facilities needs to be expanded. This will ultimately result in substantial cost savings for the hotel sector and will contribute to better awareness of the public in general of environmental measures which can, and hopefully in the future will, be taken to attain sustainable tourism development.

12 As tourism is an information-intensive industry, its success depends on the educational level of host communities. Improving access to, and the quality of, basic education in destination areas should therefore be a priority. Likewise, extensive investment in professional training and capacity building at local level is essential to ensure equitable distribution of its benefits to local populations.

13 Improving and building on existing information and understanding is an important aspect of resource management for sustainable development. A comprehensive and multidisciplinary scientific research programme in all aspects of tourism, supported by well-established and globally linked institutions, is part of any sustainable tourism development plan. Evaluation and review also are essential parts of the cycle of monitoring programmes. This helps to keep programmes 'on track', allow adjustments to be made in light of changing circumstances, and help to guide the efficient and effective use of both the public and private sector resources.

14 Sustainability indicators are useful tools. They are helpful in linking monitoring programmes with the evaluation process and, when linked to targets, they provide criteria by which to judge progress.

15 The conference endorses the proposed UNEP "Principles for Implementation of Sustainable Tourism", the WTO Global Code of Ethics for Tourism, and the Dakar Principles for Tourism in World Heritage Areas.

16 The underlying message of the conference therefore is that a viable, diverse and competitive tourism industry cannot be developed, and certainly not sustained, without giving full attention to the above three subject areas. Improving the quality of life and developing an economically viable and sustainable nature, heritage and community-based tourism industry are, in fact, mutually dependent upon, and supportive of, protecting the Region's resources.

17 As societies develop, our 'window' to the world is becoming larger. If we are to live together in the same global community of the future we must learn to accept each other's differences, be tolerant of each other's beliefs, become knowledgeable about each other's values. Through tourism we can promote interaction, friendship, increase awareness of environmental protection and promote the future prospects of world peace.

18 Finally, the Conference recognised that Hainan Province has a wide spectrum of tourism resources that can be converted into sustainable tourism products, benefiting a large proportion of the local population. It also noted the opportunity offered by the forthcoming Hainan Master Plan for Sustainable Tourism Development to be executed by the World Tourism Organisation, and the need to implement its recommendations.

19 The Conference participants expressed their thanks to WTO, UNEP, UNESCO, the Hainan Provincial Government and the Chinese Tourism authorities for the excellent hospitality and facilities given to make this Conference a success.

Chapter VIII (Tourism Resources) of Programme of Action for the Suustainable Development of Small Island Developing State

Basis for Action

Tourism has contributed much to the development of small island developing States and, as one of only a few development options for those small States, will continue to be very important for their future growth. It could also stimulate the development of other sectors. However, if not properly planned and managed, tourism could significantly degrade the environment on which it is so dependent. The fragility and interdependence of coastal zones and the unspoilt areas on which eco-tourism depends calls for careful management. One of the special tourist attractions of small island developing States is the distinctiveness of their cultures. The diversity and fragility of their environments are reflected in the diversity and fragility of their cultures. The protection of the former is an important condition for the protection of the latter.

Capital investment in tourism, particularly for the necessary infrastructure, is costly. There is usually great competition for land resources among tourism, agriculture and other land uses. Large increases in tourism and the overdevelopment of tourism in particular areas or in whole islands could be environmentally and culturally disruptive and detrimental to other valuable sectors, such as agriculture. It is imperative, therefore, that the development of tourism be carefully planned, particularly in relation to compatible land uses, water management, coastal zone management and the development of parks and protected areas. Tourism, like all forms of development in the coastal zone, needs to be carefully integrated within the existing cultural and environmental constraints and opportunities present within small island developing States. Eco-tourism, linking areas of high ecological value to low-impact tourism, may present important and environmentally sustainable opportunities for tourism development in small island developing States.

A. National action, policies and measures

(i) Ensure that tourism development and environmental management are mutually supportive.

(ii) Adopt integrated planning and policies to ensure sustainable tourism development, with particular attention to land-use planning and coastal zone management, requiring environmental impact assessments for all tourism projects; the continuous monitoring of the environmental impact of all tourism activities; and the development of guidelines and standards for design and construction taking into account energy and water consumption, the generation and disposal of wastes and land degradation, the proper management and protection of eco-tourism attractions, and the carrying capacity of areas for tourism.

(iii) Identify and develop facilities to meet specific niche markets, particularly in eco-tourism, nature and cultural tourism, and involve local populations in the identification and management of natural protected areas set aside for eco-tourism.

(iv) Adopt measures to protect the cultural integrity of small island developing States.

B. Regional action

(i) Ensure that tourism and the environment are mutually supportive in cooperation schemes at the regional level including, where appropriate, through harmonizing standards and regulations.

(ii) Encourage the assessment and development of potential complementarities among small island developing States, including the development of packaged options covering several islands and joint marketing and training programmes.

(iii) Establish or strengthen regional mechanisms for the exchange of information on the development of a safe and sustainable tourism sector, using, as appropriate, the capacities of regional tourism organizations.

C. International action

(i) Promote the recognition by the international community of both the value of tourism in small island developing States and the fragility of the resources on which it depends, and of the resulting need for international support to encourage its sustainable development.

(ii) Facilitate efforts, at the national and regional levels, to assess the overall impact of the economic, social and ecological aspects of tourism, plan sustainable tourism and to develop eco- and cultural tourism.

7

International Conference On Sustainable Tourism In Small Island Developing States (SIDS) And Other Islands

INTRODUCTION

The International Conference on Sustainable Tourism in Small Island Developing States (SIDS) and Other Islands was convened and held jointly by the World Tourism Organization (WTO) and the United Nations Environment Programme (UNEP) in Lanzarote, Spain, from 25 to 28 October 1998.

The Conference had a twofold aim: first, to examine the development of the tourism sector in SIDS and other islands and to evaluate the progress made in the implementation of the "Programme of Action for the Sustainable Development of Small Island Developing States", formulated at the Barbados Conference of 1994; and, second, to provide guidelines and recommendations to the Commission for Sustainable Development (CSD) of the United Nations for the revision of the aforementioned Barbados Programme of Action to be undertaken by the General Assembly in 1999.

Part-1 Summary of main Conclusions and Recommendations

Recommendations at the National Level

— tourism in SIDS should be considered as only one of the components of, and be fully integrated into, the overall sustainable development of the island;

— the challenges and opportunities for tourism development in the middle term and possible long-term scenarios should be considered;

— sustainable tourism in SIDS will require a change in mentality of all stakeholders in tourism development and management. It is thus essential that awareness campaigns and educational programmes be developed to reach the various stakeholders.

Sustainable development policy and planning

— planning should be based on a sound knowledge of, and take into account the conservation of, the natural and cultural resources of the island. In particular, fragile and richly endowed biodiversity ecosystems such as coral reefs and mangroves, and social values of the local communities should be considered;

— an integrated approach for the management of all resources and in particular coastal zones should be adopted;

— SIDS should consider the environmental and socio-cultural carrying capacity of the island in their tourism policy and strategy;

— all stakeholders and, in particular, local communities should be involved in the definition, planning and implementation of the sustainable tourism development policy and plan.

Tourism development and management

— local communities should be involved and reap benefits from tourism, and public and private partnerships developed;

— when applicable, not only the development but also the rehabilitation of tourism facilities and services should be considered;.

— sustainable tourism in SIDS will require the development and adoption of alternative designs of tourism facilities, according to the characteristics of each island and with a view to ensuring a sustainable use of their natural resources. In particular, the use of renewable energy should be considered:

— development and adoption of ecoefficiency and cleaner production strategies and policies will also be required;

— the possibility and viability of introducing environmentally sound technologies should be considered;

— voluntary codes of conduct, industry standards and ecolabels should be adapted and tailored to suit particularities of SIDS; the promotion of best practices should be developed.

Monitoring of impacts

The monitoring of impacts is a necessary condition for sustainable development. This is even more important in

SIDS given the characteristics of their natural and cultural environment. It is thus essential that SIDS:

— identify and develop sets of indicators for sustainable tourism in their countries contributing towards measuring sustainability;

— develop observatories of sustainable tourism development.

Recommendations at the Regional Level

Due to their small size and isolation, regional co-operation is one of the important conditions for sustainable development of SIDS. In particular:

— environmental regulations and standards should be harmonized for SIDS in the same region;

— voluntary industry codes, standards and ecolabels should also be considered, whenever possible, at the regional level;

— exchange of experience and dissemination of good practices from the social, environmental and economic points of view should be developed between SIDS from the same region;

— raising awareness campaigns and capacity building activities should be launched at the regional level whenever possible;

— SIDS could consider joining forces for facilitating the funding of sustainable tourism projects and activities.

Regional and international organizations should encourage and assist in this regional co-operation.

Recommendations at the International Level

International organizations, and in particular UNEP and WTO should :

— encourage SIDS to ratify, if not already done, international and regional conventions and help them to fulfil their commitments under these conventions (Regional Seas Conventions, Convention on Biological Diversity, World Heritage Site Convention, Montreal Protocol etc.);

— assist with the development and implementation of :

  — transfer of technology and know-how and more widely with sustainable development approaches in the tourism sector;

  — voluntary approaches such as codes of conduct and ecolabels;

  — indicators and observatories;

  — develop exchange of experiences at the international level on sustainable tourism in SIDS;

  — better disseminate existing pilot projects and good practices;

— develop or participate in raising awareness campaigns and capacity building activities for sustainable tourism.

As a direct follow-up of the Conference, UNEP and WTO should:

— jointly prepare and disseminate case studies of sustainable tourism in SIDS, based among others on the examples presented in the working groups at the Lanzarote conference;

— consider jointly convening regular meetings at the international and/ or regional levels, to discuss the various issues and possible solutions relating to sustainable tourism in SIDS.

Part-2: Key Issues for Sustainable Tourism in SIDS and Other Islands

1. Islands and SIDS are extremely fragile integrated systems whose future development needs to be focused on sustainable and integrated options capable of reconciling the economy, human development and environmental conservation.

2. Tourism is a booming sector, with a strong capacity for transforming fragile environments, which constitutes both an opportunity and a challenge for islands and SIDS: an opportunity to diversify limited economic activities and employment in the islands, and a challenge, as tourism has considerable impacts on island systems, usually extremely vulnerable. These impacts need to be fully taken into account and properly managed.

3. Sustainable tourism development (STD) is becoming, all over the world and hence in SIDS and other islands, an irrevocable and irreversible demand on the part of tourists and local populations. Growing demands are made for quality surroundings in which environmental sustainability, nature, culture, exceptional places with an identity of their own and authenticity are considered to be key values in terms of tourism appeal and local quality of life. Thus, a positive interaction should be sought between tourism and environmental, socio-cultural and economic factors.

4. The viability of new sustainable tourism policies in SIDS and other islands is becoming increasingly conditioned by the very broad participation of all stakeholders. In particular, it will be impossible to multiply the economic effects of tourism, achieve positive social and cultural development or conserve island ecosystems and natural resources without making the local community jointly responsible for meeting these aims.

5. In order to steer tourism and island development towards sustainability, criteria, instruments and lines of action must be established and implemented forthwith. The "carrying capacity" of the island system in relation to tourism is all-important, and integrated long-term strategies must be introduced as a preventive measure. Delaying the application of sustainable policies until the emergence of problems of economic downturn and cultural or environmental degradation can make it very difficult, even unfeasible, to correct these processes.

6. Tourism development in SIDS and other islands is presently characterised by its expansive potential and by the unequal situation of islands and regions. In the last four years, 90% of SIDS have seen an increase in visitor numbers, but the regions of Africa and Asia/ Pacific encompass the states which are finding it more difficult to make their corresponding tourism sectors take off.

7. On the other hand, in SIDS and other islands which are trying to launch or strengthen their tourism development, there is an overriding concern with problems which limit tourism growth in the short term - mainly air access, capital and infrastructure. The need

to introduce sustainability criteria geared to preventing the emergence of serious socio-cultural and environmental imbalances in island systems in the future is not perceived as important yet.

8. In SIDS and other islands which have reached maturity without adopting sustainability criteria, problems which are difficult to resolve tend to arise in connection with the obsolescence and congestion of the tourism product, the poor economic integration of tourism in the island, the increasing degradation of the environment, and growing social intolerance towards tourism and imported labour.

9. In recent years, and particularly as a result of the Rio Conference in 1992 and the Barbados Conference in 1994, there has been evidence that various measures are being developed in SIDS and other islands trying to improve the integration of tourism in sustainable island development. Nonetheless, inter-island cooperation and information is still very weak and generally there is a shortage of specific knowledge and suitable indicators to evaluate the real situation. Available analyses do not incorporate the implications of the various levels of island development, and real experiences, which could expedite progress in STD in SIDS and other islands, are barely being divulged outside their territory.

Key Action Areas at State and Island Level for Promoting Sustainable Tourism and Island Development

A suitable institutional, legal framework and strategy

10. Set up, at the outset, an institutional and legal framework and strategy in line with the principles of

STD, and with the characteristics and development level of each SIDS or island. More precisely, the jurisdictional capacities of island states constitute an extraordinary opportunity to institutionalise from the outset the sustainability of tourism policies. The possibility of establishing incentives and eco-taxes to reward good practices, boost the conservation of valuable resources and discourage undesirable impacts should be more widely considered.

11. Verify, from the outset the different tourism strategies and future scenarios. Consider the compatibility of economic, socio-cultural and environmental factors, and adopt those scenarios which are conducive to strengthening, at a suitable pace, sustainable options for the medium and long term. In this respect, the STD of SIDS and other islands can hinge on overcoming the attraction for swift and unlimited growth. The possibility to accommodate foreign-visitor affluence through flexible planning of the tourism product and the suitable management of gates of access to each island - ports and airports - should be considered.

12. Gear the tourism strategy towards the values and carrying capacities of each island, and towards the integration of a multi-thematic product which is as genuine, rich and diverse as possible. Preserve natural resources; extend the scope of tourism attractions; and increase the yields of tourism investments, stabilize employment, and rationalize the management of environmental resources. If appropriate, develop a product which is as deseasonalized as possible, if this helps to prevent human pressures on the environment.

13. Seek, right from the start, a broad island consensus relative to the preparation and development of

sustainable tourism strategies and policies. Develop fora based on institutional leadership, consultation with private players and partnership with social representatives. These fora provide an opportunity to establish joint agreements, as well as to negotiate solutions to conflicts between the different visions and interests of each social group.

Integrated and preventive tourism planning

14. Develop instruments for preventive, concerted and flexible planning and management - Agenda 21, Integrated Tourism Plans, or other similar plans - which contribute to maximizing the integration of tourism in the island system, and define the extent and marshal the tourism development of each SIDS or island.

15. Make tourism compatible with the conservation of the main ecosystems (coral reefs, mangrove forests, land forests...), bio-diversity and natural resources. This requires the integration of tourism in regional planning and development geared to conserving the island's most valuable natural, rural and urban sites. The creation of Parks and Protected Sites is a suitable and compatible measure which serves to increase the value of tourism in the islands.

16. Anticipate measures for the conservation and sustainable development of the most vulnerable areas and those under the most pressure, particularly coastal zones, where specific coastal management plans and integrated systems should be developed. Assess tourism projects, create "coastal reserves", conserve coastal ecosystems and bio-diversity, harmonize the

coexistence of tourism with all the other activities, and establish a mutually beneficial relationship with the interior of the island.

17. Pay special attention to making tourism compatible with the conservation-valuation of the historical-cultural heritage of each island, considering not only its protection for preventive purposes, but also its possible recovery as a responsibly managed tourism resource which is open to the local population.

18. Suitably evaluate the socio-cultural impact and population mobility generated by new tourism developments, and responsibly marshal and adjust their scale, rhythm and level of integration in the islands' urban infrastructure through regional planning and the programming of the corresponding tourism product in the different areas.

19. Suitably regulate the creation of new coastal facilities and nautical tourism activities. In the first case, this involves making a preliminary evaluation of any activity which, like sports centres, marinas, etc., is liable to distort the coastal dynamics with unpredictable long-term effects; in the second, it involves regulating activities which, like diving, fishing, etc., may have a negative effect on the conservation of habitats and the bio-diversity of island coasts.

20. Forestall the possible decline of the mature tourism coastal zones by promoting Concerted Integral Rehabilitation Plans with the local community and the private sector: improved integration in the surroundings, the modernization and diversification of the tourism product, the recovery of urban and

environmental quality, restoration of tourism installations and marketing of a new image.

21. Promote and regulate appropriate siting and design procedures, introduce impact prevention instruments, and in particular Environmental Impact Assessment for tourism projects, and standards and incentives to promote responsible tourism, in particular, the reduction of resources consumption and generation of waste.

A sustainable orientation of the main policies and programmes of action: accessibility, economic resources, infrastructures and training

22. Define key policies for STD in each SIDS or island (investment capital, infrastructure, water plan, environmental protection...) together with new priorities and programmes of action. Consider the suitability of creating a Sustainable Tourism Development Agency in association with the private sector, in order to implement these policies and programmes.

23. Design a feasible and sustainable island access strategy (air and sea). In many islands poor access is undermining a balanced tourism development. All the possibilities for globalising and restructuring air transport must be gauged with a view to improving access to each island. In other islands which may be subject to excessive tourist pressure, suitably controlled and selective access is all-important in terms of preventing the carrying capacities of these islands from being exceeded. In all events, the islands should be aware that long-distance tourist arrivals generate an environmental bill for CO_2 emissions and other gases

with significant greenhouse effects. It is therefore necessary to combine the application of environmentally-responsible island policies with the procurement of international recognition of their exceptional dependence on transport to and from the island.

24. Make available the financial resources required for island tourism development, combining direct and indirect government action, joint measures with island private initiative, and scanning regional and international public and private banks for foreign capital. Promote linkages between tourism and the other economic sectors (including agriculture and fisheries), promoting a broad network of small and medium-sized local companies which multiply the economic spin-offs of tourism, extend the number of available small-scale services, and actively and beneficially integrate the local population. It should not be forgotten that the multiplier effect of tourism expenditure is economically, socially and environmentally far more interesting than the mere growth in visitor numbers.

25. Prior and flexible planning of investment in, and regulation of, tourism infrastructures to make them viable and ensure that they go hand in hand with tourism development, contribute their synergies with relation to island development, and minimize undesirable impacts. Refrain from attempting to resolve any excess in the destination's carrying capacity by simply increasing the number of infrastructures, since this will only contribute to magnifying degradation processes in the future.

26. Promote and undertake the training of entrepreneurial, professional and labour human resources at the private and public levels related with STD in SIDS and other islands. Analyse existing training programmes and facilities to define the gaps and necessary actions.

A responsible management of natural resources

27. Incorporate from the outset the tourism impact relative to key environmental factors in terms of their effect on the island environment (useful land, mobility, water, energy, materials, waste...), in global environmental problems (global warming, depletion of the ozone layer, the loss of biodiversity...); furthermore link tourism development to the sustainable planning and management of these factors in order to ensure its positive integration into their corresponding environments.

28. Design tourism strategies and projects which make provisions for a good relationship between the mobility they require and the impacts and costs they generate, placing priority on reducing movements and increasing the proximity of the services required, and providing incentives for voluntary use of collective transport for long distances and walking and cycling for short distances.

29. Establish and supervise water quality in the main bathing areas of the island, and design reliable information and certification systems, ideally integrated and with common criteria at regional level.

30. Conceive the use of water resources for tourism purposes in a zone, considering the "complete water cycle", bearing in mind its priority uses in that zone, and introducing suitable measures for obtaining water

(paying attention to aquifers and natural courses), ensuring water quality, saving, efficiency, purification, reuse, and clean spillage; all this is to be done in such a way that the new tourism projects not only do not increase water problems in the area but also contribute to resolving them. Avoid massive recourse to the desalination of sea water on account of the ensuing cost and energy bills.

31. Reduce energy consumption and control corresponding emissions in tourism projects: use of renewable energy (solar, wind...), bio-climatic design of construction projects, energy savings and increased efficiency of facilities in installations, etc.

32. Evaluate the effect of the waste generated by tourism developments and adopt solutions which do not destabilise existing waste management systems in each zone: reduce waste generation; avoid uncontrolled dumping; introduce selective waste collection, treatment and recycling systems; and reduce to a minimum and suitably manage the remaining waste fraction.

33. Adapt tourism constructions to the surroundings and local conditions by applying aesthetic criteria, bio-climatic design, use of suitable materials, and the application of systems and installations which reduce consumption of resources which are in short supply and the generation of undesirable emissions (CFCs, CO_2, N_2O, CH_4).

A commitment to environmental awareness, voluntary collaboration, and the monitoring of island development

34. The promotion of social awareness-raising campaigns regarding STD among all sectors and players directly

and indirectly involved in tourism, is an indispensable requirement for tackling the cultural change it requires. These campaigns should be coordinated and disseminated in line with the characteristics of their specific audiences: tourism entrepreneurs, visitors, workers, general public, training centres.

35. Promote codes of conduct for sustainable tourism among all stakeholders in the tourism sector.

36. Promote the introduction of eco-labels as a tool for sustainable tourism.

37. Promote eco-audits and environmental quality management systems in the tourism sector (hotels, golf courses, marinas, etc) and make provisions to incorporate them in island regulations.

38. Monitor, on a permanent basis, the development of the main parameters related to tourism, quality of life and island sustainability, by creating island observatories which publicly and periodically evaluate the main indicators of the island system, and gauge the extent to which institutional programmes meet the aforementioned objectives.

Key Action Areas at Regional Level for Promoting Sustainable Tourism and Island Development

39. Cooperation should be developed among islands in the same geographical region.

40. The boundaries of these regions should be based on common economic, cultural, political interests and goals, so that their delimitation is really operative.

41. Regional activities could include:

— regional regulations and trans-boundary marine reserves;

— fora on topics related with STD at regional level, the extension of common tourism policies and accreditation of standards, indicators, incentives and eco-taxes, etc, and draft voluntary codes of conduct and quality labels which contribute to improving and promoting an environmentally responsible image among tourism consumers;

— services of common interest: information and contacts, multi-thematic technical support, a data bank of good practices, technical and sustainable management consultancy;

— training courses and cycles for entrepreneurs, public servants and professionals;

— inter-island networks to foster the exchange of experiences;

— common marketing activities, entrepreneurial joint ventures, and contact with financial institutions.

Key Action Areas at International Level for Promoting Sustainable Tourism and Island Development

42. The international framework of SIDS and other islands is crucial in terms of evaluating situations and scenarios, formulating policies, facilitating access to resources, and developing guidelines from an international tourism perspective. One cannot lose sight of the present globalization process, nor of the fact that many of the major agreements and guidelines which affect SIDS are formulated at international fora, both institutional, mainly UN, and private, big business associations, investment funds.

43. At the international level, there are many organizations and institutions that have connections with SIDS, other

islands and their sustainable development. Mention should be made of the following on account of their influence and operative importance: AOSIS, the SIDS Alliance, the UN and its departments and agencies (UNEP, UNDP, UNESCO and various others), the World Bank and regional development banks; and the World Tourism Organization. A Guide of functions and programmes on sustainable tourism development programmes at the international level should be promoted.

44. Many activities can be promoted and developed at the international level which include:

— Programme of proposals and initiatives to be presented to the international community, and the drafting of broad international agreements, related with STD in SIDS and other islands.

— Analyses, indicators, statistics, forecasting and strategic guidelines on tourism and sustainable development in SIDS and other islands.

— The holding of an International Conference and the awarding of a World Prize every two or three years with the presentation of a Report-Balance-Guidelines on STD in SIDS and other islands.

— High-level training for tourism professionals and other players in SIDS, and theoretical and practical courses and seminars on key aspects of sustainable tourism planning and management in the islands.

— Development of an information programme via Internet with basic contents and "good STD practices":

— Technical support and promotion of STD Demo-Projects.

Conclusions and Recommendations of the Working Gorups

Working group No. 1 reached the following conclusions and recommendations:

1. It is clear that in the formulation of tourism and environmental development plans, it is vital to incorporate the participation of all stakeholders, and particularly the local communities. The incorporation of all stakeholders for consensus building has proven to be a key ingredient for success in several examples we studied in our group. Furthermore, participation should occur at all levels (from start to finish).
2. It is also important to begin thinking about formulating plans which look beyond the traditional 5, 10, 15 or 20 year planning horizons.
3. As it was demonstrated in the presentation on Cuba, governments can play a more active role in favoring new investments which not only meet their environmental requirements, but ones which go beyond and demonstrate more initiative. Companies which demonstrate environmental initiative should receive more recognition and reward from their governments.
4. Cooperation both within governments (between relevant ministries and agencies) and between governments (regionally and internationally) is vital.
5. International and regional organizations can play an important role in better assisting in the transfer of technology and knowhow and play a larger role in assisting in funding facilitation for small tourism projects.

6. Private sector operators should play an increasing role in educating their clients on environmental issues. Several operators have demonstrated how doing this can help tourism destinations to improve their environmental standards and encourage better environmental practices.

Working group No 2 reached the following conclusions and recommendations:

1. Recognizing the fact that sustainable tourism is about continuous education with all stakeholders, the need arises for the implementation of awareness campaigns and educational programmes, so that the investment is focused on people not only physical development.

2. To safeguard the integrity of SIDS environments through an interdisciplinary approach, recognizing the importance of the interlinkages and functions of coastal and inland ecosystems.

3. To develop and adopt alternative designs of tourism facilities according to the characteristics of SIDS considering the viability of introducing sound environmental technologies.

4. To establish concrete mechanisms to fully handle conflicting interests whilst seeking to improve collaboration and the building of partnerships.

5. To promote the involvement and commitment of local communities in tourism development and decision making by building co-ownership and development of self-reliance processes such as in the case of the Soufrière Marine Management Area.

6. To assist in the reporting of the state of conservation of sites and cultural centres through research and on-

going campaigns, recognising the World Heritage listing as a valuable tool for sustainable tourism development.

7. To develop tools such as codes of conduct, and promote best management practices as a means of contributing towards a sustainable tourism industry, bearing in mind the need for clear target audiences and a bottom-up approach.

8. To determine and monitor the environmental, socio and economic impacts of cruises, taking into account issues related to current trends in the cruise industry, such as destination oriented cruises versus megaships as destinations in their own right.

9. To promote tourism development that takes into account the environmental as well as the socio-cultural carrying capacities through the establishment of flexible threshholds.

10. To develop a set of tourism indicators to be used as comparative tools contributing towards measuring sustainability in small island States.

11. To promote information technology that can play a role through software packages such as GIS, in providing land use information that can also be used as a tool for planning, policy setting and management in SIDS.

12. To ensure that socio-cultural, environmental and economic costs are taken into account prior to developing tourism facilities, and that the combined costs do not outweigh any benefits to be accrued from such a proposed development.

Global Conclusion

Working Group 2 feels that this Conference should be an initiation of a process which needs to be taken up. Regular meetings would be much more fruitful than having a one-off meeting to discuss the various issues and problems relating to SIDS.

Working group No 3 reached the following conclusions and recommendations:

Pre-requisites

1 Sustainable Tourism must take place within a framework and content of nation development and linked to all other sectors, productive or otherwise

2. Juxtapositioning of economic development, social equity and environmental sustainability.

3. Sustainable tourism initiatives must be economically viable and internationally competitive

4. Adequate financial and human resources

5. Adequate air transportation

General comments

Sustainable tourism must be planned within a well articulated strategy:

— Intersectoral

— Community participation

— Integrated planning

— Sustainable use of natural resources

— Identify mitigation for possible impacts of various forms of proposed tourism

— Set up an Action Programme

— Identify indicators for monitoring goals and objective of strategy

— Identify appropriate institutional mechanisms for implementing strategy

Some selected tools for Sustainable Tourism are:

— Parks and Protected Areas

— Environmental standards and regulations - these standards should be harmonised for SIDS in a similar region

— Industry Standards e.g. ecolabelling, should be adapted and tailored to suit peculiarities of regional SIDS

— Community participation in the planning, development and management of sustainable tourism initiatives

— Limits of acceptable charge - carry capacity

— Industry certification - ecoefficiency, cleaner production.

The involvement of host communities and communities in buffer zones to touristic sites is very important. The issues that arise are:

1 How to mobilise the community

2. Processes for community involvement:

 — community development

 — training

 — entrepreneurial developments

 — access to funding

3. Economic viability of community based tourism

Bibliography

Briguglio, L. Butler, R. Harrison, D. Filho, W. (eds) 'Sustainable Tourism in Islands and Small States: Case Studies', Pinter: UK, HB, 1855673711 stlg45.00, 1996

_______________, Archer, B., Jafari, J. and Wall, G. (eds) 'Sustainable Tourism in Islands and Small States: Issues and Policies', Pinter: UK, HB, ISBN 1855673703 stlg45.00, 1996

Conlin, M. and Baum, T. (eds) 'Island Tourism: Management Principles and Practice', Wiley: UK, HB, ISBN 0471955566 stlg50.00, 1995

King, B. 'Creating Island Resorts', Routledge: UK, HB, ISBN 0415149894 stlg50.00, 1998

King, B., Tourism higher education in island microstates, Tourism Management, 15(4), pp. 267-272, 1994.

Lockhart, D.G. and Drakakis-Smith, D. (eds) 'Island Tourism: Trends and Prospects', Pinter: UK, HB, ISBN 1855674165 stlg57.50, 1996

Shareef, R., 'Small Island Tourism Economies: A Bird's Eye View', in D. Post (ed.), *Proceedings of the International Conference on Modelling and Simulation:Socio-economic Systems,* Townsville, Australia, 3, 1124-1129, 2003

Index